The Romantic Road

from the River Main to the Alps

Text: Wolfgang Kootz

Fotography: W. Sauer, U. Strauch and others

Kraichgau Verlag

The Romantic Road - the most famous and well known touristic route

This small book will be your guide and companion, whether you intend to explore the Romantic Road in its entirety - all 350 kilometres, excluding the short excursions off to one side - or in separate stages. (We Germans call it „Romantic“ because that is our word for the old castles, unspoilt villages, and lovely natural countryside beloved of poets of the „romantic“ period.) Whilst we describe the 26 cities, towns, and villages which are members of this group fairly extensively, in proportion to their size and importance, the numerous sights worth seeing a short distance away from the main route are mentioned only briefly; they are intended as recommended additions to the „compulsory programme“. A plan of the old city centre is included for the larger towns and cities to help you find your way through the often twisty, narrow streets and to track down the cultural and artistic highlights of this tourist route. As it is usually very easy to reach these places on the motorway or the main roads, tourists staying in the vicinity should allow themselves time to explore this, the oldest and most famous of the German tourist routes, providing as it does as cross-section through diverse landscapes and offering a wealth of culture the visitor would never have imagined. Behind the walls of old Imperial and dynastic cities, half-timbered houses and wine-making villages, there are oases of peace and quiet inviting the passer-by to stay and rest far from the main north-south trunk roads. Although this book is mainly designed to suit the tourist in a car, it can of course be used by those who arrive by bus or rail.

Right from its start-point in Würzburg, which boasts the Marienburg, the Käppele, the old bridge over the River Main, the cathedral, and first and foremost the residential palace of the Prince-Bishops, the Romantic Road offers the visitor a cornucopia of historic artistic treasures. This is the capital of the Franconian Main region, and here artists like Riemenschneider, Neumann, and Tiepolo created immortal masterpieces which often radiate their beauty into other towns and villages in the district. The region to the south is the Baden part of Franconia, with the charming valley of the River Tauber and its sunny vineyards around Tauberbischofsheim and Lauda-Königshofen. The richness of the works of arts in its churches and the innumerable statues of saints and of the Saviour have given this district the name of Madonnenländchen, the „Little Madonna-land“; it is also famous for its unspoilt natural beauty and the diversity of its flora and fauna.

The charm of the Romantic Road also stems from the large number of minor rulers, both spiritual and worldly, that used to reside here. The High Masters of the Deutscher Orden, an Order of chivalry, left their castle to posterity in Bad Mergentheim , as did the powerful Lords of Hohenlohe in Weikersheim.

The route leads through Röttingen and Creglingen and one of the most charming of river valleys to Rothenburg ob der Tauber, the quintessence of romantic medieval towns. This is the start of a long line of former Free Imperial Cities running through Feuchtwangen, Dinkelsbühl, and Nördlingen to Donauwörth. Their historic town centres are, without exception, so well preserved that you might think that history had held its breath here. In between these towns there are the minor residences of the Princes of Hohenlohe-Schillingsfürst and of Oettingen-Wallerstein providing variety just as much as does the massive Harburg castle, high above the Wörnitz valley between the Swabian and the Franconian Alb. South of the Danube we travel through the Donauried and reach Augsburg, a city 2,000 years old and once the centre of the trading empires of the Fugger and the Welser merchant dynasties. This is where the painter Holbein the Elder worked, and the architect Elias Holl, where Protestants and Catho-

lics signed their peace treaty in 1555, and where every step we take brings us face to face with testimony of the city's grand historical past. A little way to one side of our route is Friedberg, once the fortified city of the Bavarian Wittelsbach royal dynasty.
Whereas the Romantic Road up to now has run more or less along the medieval trading road through Würzburg, from Augsburg onwards it runs mainly along the line of the Roman military road, the via claudia, which once linked Augsburg with Rome. It runs across the Lechfeld, the battlefield where Otto the Great defeated the Hungarians in 955 and thus drove them out of Central Europe. We visit Landsberg and Hohenfurch before reaching Schongau and entering the Pfaffenwinkel, a region that is almost an open-air museum in its own right with monasteries and churches containing the inimitable paintings and stucco work of the great Wessobrunn masters. The highpoint is the most beautiful rococo church in the world, the Wieskirche. In terms of public interest, its only rivals are the royal Bavarian castles near Schwangau: the romantically extended Hohenschwangau and, opposite it, King Ludwig II's fairy-tale castle of Neuschwanstein.
Even Nature played some of the notes in the closing chord of the Romantic Road, contributing meadows and forests, and lakes and chains of mountains, as the back-drop to these magnificent buildings. The route finally ends in Füssen, in the eastern Allgäu, only a stone's throw from the Austrian border.
Anyone who has travelled along this magnificent tourist route with eyes open to see the almost inexhaustible wealth of our cultural inheritance will be thankful that our forefathers have bequeathed such a plethora of works of art to us, and for this reason our generation is likewise called upon to do everything we can to preserve this rich heritage and to pass it on intact to posterity.

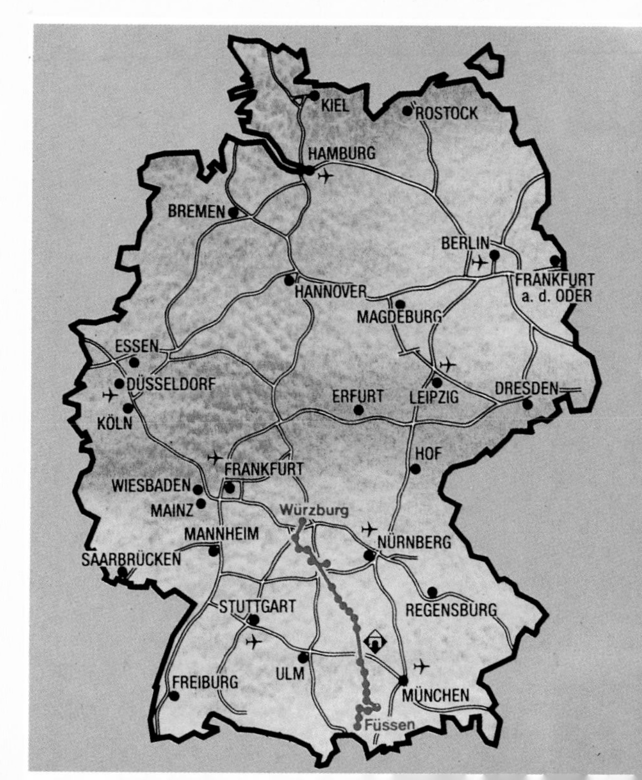

Germany, showing the main motorway routes. The Romantic Road has been added with special emphasis.

Würzburg

The „Romantic Road" starts in Würzburg with a fanfare. The former seat of the Prince-Bishops possesses a cornucopia of cultural treasures of international importance, despite all the destruction of the 1945 air raid, and in 1982 the Residential Palace was added to the UNESCO World Heritage List.

The settlement on the banks of the Main was mentioned in records as long ago as

The massive castle of Marienberg above the vineyards was once the residence of the Prince-Bishops of Würzburg. In the foreground is the Old Main bridge.

Congress and Tourism Centre, *Am Congress Centrum, 97070 Würzburg, Phone +49 931/372335, Fax +49 931/373652, Internet: http://www.wuerzburg.de, e-mail: tourismus@wuerzburg.de*
Residence: *April-October Tues.-Sun. 9:00 am - 5:00 pm; November-March Tues.-Sun. 10:00 am - 16:00 pm, Phone +49 931/3551712.*
Martin-von-Wagner Museum in the Residance: Art Gallery *Tues.-Sat. 9:30 am - 12:30 pm*
Antique Collection *Tues.-Sat. 2:00-5:00 pm, Sun. (Art Collection or Antique Collection) 9:30 am - 12.30 pm -* ***Graphics Collection*** *Tues. and Thurs. 4:00 - 6:00 pm, admission free, phone +49 931/312288. -* ***Fortress Marienburg:*** *grounds are open for viewing year round. -* ***Mainfränkisches Museum:*** *April-Oct. Tues.-Sun. 10:00 am - 5:00 pm, Nov.-March Tues.-Sun. 10:00 am - 16:00 pm, phone +49 931/43016.*
Fuerstenbaumuseum: *April-Sept. Tues.-Sun. 9:30 am - 12:30 pm + 1:00 - 5:00 pm, Oct.-March Tues.-Sun. 10:00 am - 12:30 pm + 1:00 - 4:00 pm, phone +49 931/43838 -* ***St. Killiansdom:*** *Easter until All Saints' Day Mon.-Sat. 10:00 am - 5:00 pm, Sun./Fr. 1:00 - 6:00 pm, All Saints' Day until Easter Mon.-Sat. 10:00 am - Noon and 2:00 - 5:00 pm, Sun./Fr. 12:30 - 1:30 pm and 2:30 - 6:00 pm -* ***Cathedral tours for individuals:*** *Mon. after Easter until All Saints' Day Mon.-Sat. at Noon, Sun./Fri. 12.30 pm; duration: approx. 1 hour.*

450 AD, and again in 650 as the citadel of Frankish dukes. It was here in 689 that the three Irish missionaries Kilian, Kolonat, and Totnan, suffered martyrdom, and in 742 that St Boniface founded the bishopric. From 1030 onwards the town belonged to the Bishops of Würzburg, who were at the same time Dukes of Franconia until Napoleon ended the worldly rule of the Church in 1802. Since then, with a short interruption from 1805 to 1814, the city has been part of Bavaria.

The first Christian church in the city, sharing with Trier cathedral the position of Germany's oldest church, was consecrated to the Glory of the Mother of God in 706, for which reason the hill on which it stands, the „Würzberg", is still called the Marienberg, as is the castle that was built on it from 1201 onwards. Until the Stadtresidenz or Residential Palace was built in the 18th century, the castle served as the prince-bishops' residence and protective shield against the citizens

1. Residential palace; 2. Marienberg castle; 3. Cathedral; 4.Neumünster; 5. St Burkard's Church; 6. Deutschhaus church; 7. Franciscan church; 8. St Mary's Chapel; 9. St Gertraud's Church; 10. Carmelite church; 11. Haug monastery; 12. St Peter's; 13. Augustinian church; 14. Käppele; 15. St Stephen's; 16. Don Bosco church; 17. St Alfons; 18. St John's; 19. Old university; 20. Juliusspital; 21. Grafeneckart and town hall; 22. Bürgerspital; 23. Old Main bridge; 24. Alter Kranen; 25. Monument; 26. Courtyards and patrician houses; 27. Conti; 28. Roter Bau (the „Red Building"); 29. Rückermainhof; 30. Huttenschlösschen; 31. Bronnbachergasse; 32. Haus Theaterstrasse; 33. Haus zum Falken; 34. Zum Rebstock; 35. Municipal gallery; 36. Otto Richter Halle; 37. Hofspital church

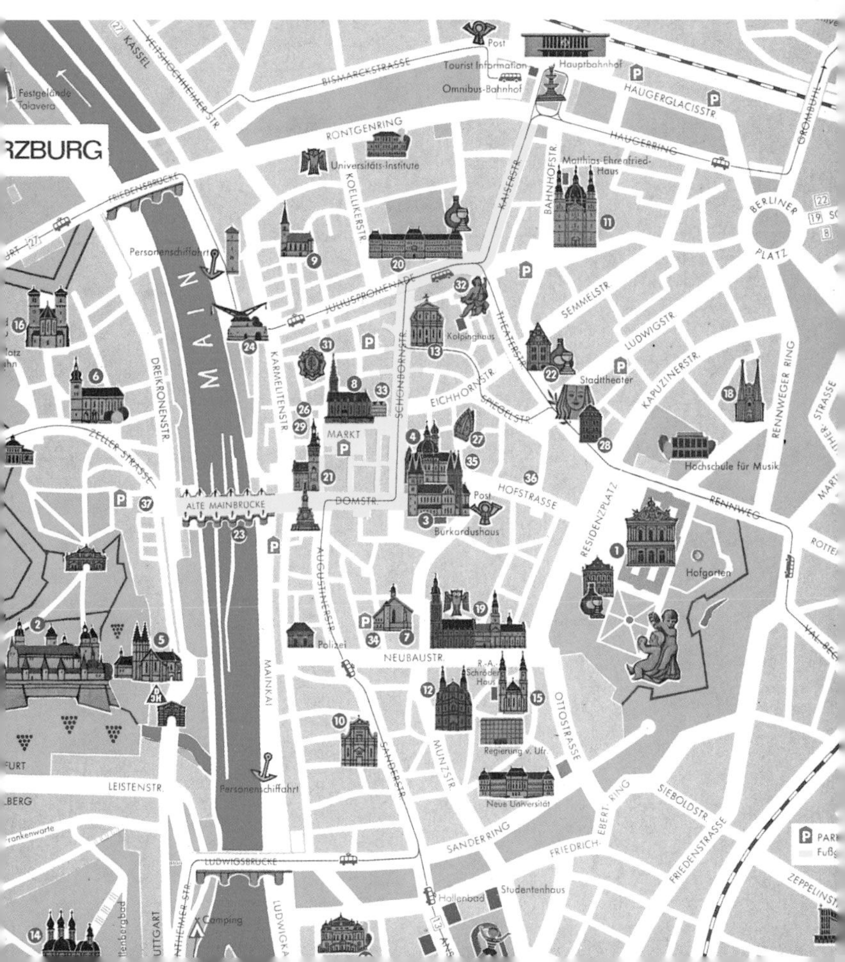

Marienberg fortress: left Kiliansturm and Scherenbergtor.

and their recurrent demands for legal freedom. It was not until 1631 that it was first conquered, by Gustav Adolf of Sweden. It was extended into an Imperial Fortress in 1642, when most of the buildings took on their present-day shape.
Nowadays they house parts of the State Archive, a small congress centre, a restaurant, the Fürstenbau museum, and the Main / Franconian Museum, which in addition to a collection of works of church art and objects bearing witness to the Franconian art of wine-growing also gives a complete view of the works of the wood-carver Tilman Riemenschneider. This famous and respected artist lived in Würzburg for 48 years and was a councillor, and later Mayor. During the Peasants' Revolt of 1525 he sided with the rebels, and after the revolt had been put down he was tortured and imprisoned. He died in 1531, a broken man, shortly after his release.
From the gardens, the visitor has a magnificent view out over the old city centre on the other side of the Main, with the Old Main bridge and the soaring towers of the old town hall, the cathedral, and the other churches and of the massive complex of the Residential Palace. The pilgrimage chapel of Käppele smiles back from its hill, the Nikolausberg, to the south; it is still visited by pious pilgrims even to this day. On the steep path up to it, terraces with chapels marking the Stations of the Cross (18th century) invite the pilgrim to rest and contemplate. The main structure of the Käppele with its onion towers was started by Balthasar Neumann, the architect of the Residential Palace, in 1748 on the basis of the pre-existing Gnadenkapelle (1653). Apart from offering a fine view, the chapel rewards the visitor with its rich interior decoration. The magnificent ceiling frescoes by Matthäus Günther, framed by the sumptuous plasterwork of the Wessobrunnen School, the organ case in the rococo style, and the classical High Altar bear witness to the diversity of styles produced in the second half of the 18th century.
The Old Main bridge leads us into the old city centre on the east bank of the Main. It took on its present-day form in the 18th and 19th centuries, although it contains masonry dating from the time

of Bishop Burkhard (8th century). Its most pleasing feature is the 12 giant baroque figures of saints and rulers. To our left soars the tower of the Grafeneckart, once the residence of a wealthy official at the Prince-Bishop's court. The two lower storeys of the building have been used as a town hall since 1316, the upper ones being added in the 15th and 16th centuries. The Wenzelsaal recalls a (not so Good) King Wenceslas who was deposed for incompetence in 1400 and bore the nickname of „Wenceslas the Lazy". In 1397, under considerable influence of alcohol, he had promised the Würzburg citizens freedom under Imperial law. Although he withdrew the promise the next day, it provoked them to rebel against the Bishop and his castle, and they were only restrained with difficulty from storming it.

Immediately behind the town hall complex, the Langgasse leads to the nearby market square with its Gothic St Mary's Chapel, built on the site of a synagogue destroyed in a pogrom in about 1400. At the market gateway we find the stone statues of Adam and Eve, the originals of which came from Riemenschneider. In the interior, the tomb of Balthasar Neumann is particularly worth seeing.

Immediately adjoining the chapel, the eye is caught by the rich stucco façade of the Falkenhaus, built in 1751 as the home of a wealthy citizen. Nowadays it accommodates the Municipal Culture Office, a Tourist Information Office, and the city library.

Just next to it stands the original Häckerbrunnen, representing an old winegrower with a pick and a wine-jug. Passing him by, we keep to the right following the Martinstrasse to the cupola of the Neumünster church. From the left-hand nave we arrive in the enchanting little Lusam garden. Under the remains of the Roman-style crossing is the epitaph of Walther von der Vogelweide, the most famous of all German Minnesängers or medieval bards. He had been granted an fiefdom in his old age from the possessions of the Neumünster monastery. The church itself is the last resting-place of the mortal remains of St Kilian, in a stone coffin.

After the church of St Mary, up on the hill, had become the seat of a Bishop in 742, the first cathedral within the city was built in 788 in the presence of Charlemagne himself. The oldest Roman-style parts of the present Cathedral of St Kilian was built at the end of the Domstrasse in about 1050. Further

Baroque stucco facade on the Falkenhaus, behind it St. Mary's Chapel.

View across the Main to the old city centre of Würzburg.
In the foreground is the Main bridge, behind it the towers of the

Grafeneckhart and the cathedral, and on the left is the cupola of the Neumünster church.

extensions and additional building followed over the course of the centuries, in the Gothic, Late Gothic, baroque, and late baroque styles.
Tombs of the bishops dating from the 12th to the 20th century decorate the church. The artistically most valuable ones are those of Prince-Bishop Rudolf von Scherenberg (died 1495) and Lorenz von Bibra (died 1519), these two being the work of Tilman Riemenschneider, and also the older gravestones of Otto von Wolfskeel (died 1345). Some of the statues are also the work of Riemenschneider's hand. The mausoleum of the bishops is still the sepulchre at the end of the south nave. This leads at its western end to the crossing (15th century), where there are further tombs dating from the 14th to the 18th century and a decorative baroque fountain.
Starting from Killiansplatz, the Hofstrasse leads between the two churches to the Residenz, a building comprising three wings categorised in 1982 by UNESCO as „World Cultural Property". The Franconia Fountain is almost lost in the wide open spaces of the Residenzplatz, which symbolises the distance between the prince and the citizens. At the foot of the column in the middle of the fountain sit Würzburg's three most famous citizens: the minstrel Walther von der Vogelweide, the painter Matthias Gothardt Neithardt alias Matthias Grünewald, and the sculptor Tilman Riemenschneider.
A conducted tour of the palace starts at the main entrance in the central building, which houses the most famous of the total of 345 rooms (not counting the gigantic wine-cellar underneath it). The architect responsible for the work, which began in 1720, was Balthasar Neumann,

The former Court Garden of the baroque Residential Palace of the Prince-Bishops with the Imperial Pavilion.

The Residential Palace: the imposing staircase with the magnificent stucco work and the famous ceiling paintings.

who succeeded in producing not only perfectly balanced architecture but also a masterpiece of structural calculation. The curved vault spanning the staircase and measuring 18 metres by 32 without any intermediate support was regarded at the time as a sensation. Its sturdy construction was put to the test during the 1945 air raid, when it was one of the few buildings to remain standing.

Not only Neumann but also the Italian painter Tiepolo achieved the climax of his creativity here, decorating the vaulted ceiling with a fresco which is the largest in the world and at the same time artistic work of the highest value. He made a symbolic representation of the four parts of the known world paying homage to the Prince-Bishops of Würzburg as the central point of the world. Here again, Neumann's vault and Tiepolo's frescoes survived the air raid unscathed. The painter here illustrated the marriage of Friedrich Barbarossa and Beatrice of Burgundy (Würzburg, 1156) and the bestowing of ducal rank on the bishop (Reichstag or imperial parliament at Würzburg in 1168). In addition to these highlights, the visitor stands amazed at the sheer magnificence of the endless sequence of rooms in late baroque and rococo, each designed in various colours and decorated with masterful stucco work. The Weisser Saal and the Gartensaal are also worth mentioning, as they contain outstanding work by Antonio Bossi. The court chapel in the south wing is also excessively ornate, but the paintings over the side-altars are from Tiepolo. This is today the favourite church for Würzburg weddings, and it is nothing unusual for 20 couples to plight their troth here in one weekend.

From the north-western corner of the Residenzplatz, the broad Theaterstrasse leads to the complex of the Bürgerspital. Endowed by wealthy Würzburg citizens in 1319, it was rebuilt many times over the centuries, but the real attraction is the enchanting inner courtyard. Passing along the Semmelstrasse and the Haugerkirchgasse, we reach towering

The Green Salon, one of the prestigious rooms.

The Residential Palace: Hall of Mirrors.

The baroque Court Chapel is the scene every week of innumerable weddings.

church of the Haug monastery, which was not including in the defensive ring around the town until the middle of the 17th century. The church (1670/71) with its 85-metre high cupola-crowned towers represents the Italian baroque period. The interior used to be richly decorated, but now only the painting above the High Altar (16th century) has been preserved.

We now follow the Haugerpfarrgasse to the Barbarossaplatz, behind which lies the broad complex of buildings making up the Juliusspital. It was created in 1576 by an endowment from the Prince-Bishop Echter von Mespelbrunn, and the endowment consisted of one of the largest wine-growing estates in Germany. Whilst part of the building nowadays houses departments of the University, in other parts there are still the „Spital" (a charity hospital) and a home for the elderly. Passing through the Fürstenbau we reach the romantic former Court Garden with its pretty baroque fountain and delightful pavilion (both dating from about 1710). The point where the Juliuspromenade meets the bank of the Main is where the bastion-like sub-structure stands of the Alte Kranen or „old crane". Balthasar Neumann's son Franz Ignaz designed this machine in about 1770. One particularly interesting point is the treadwheels of the technical monument, which can still be viewed today. About 200 metres further downstream, the Old Main bridge marks the end of our tour.

From Würzburg it is well worth making an excursion to Veitshöchheim (8 kilometres along B 27 main road), where the Prince-Bishops had a baroque summer palace built to plans by Neumann. It includes one of the most delightful court gardens in Europe, completed in 1779.

Tauberbischofsheim

Despite all the Romanticism along the banks of the Main, the Romantic Road begins in Würzburg, on the Main, but then leaves the river to follow the B 27 main road in a south-westerly direction. Its first stopping-place is in Tauberbischofsheim, where Frankish tribes have settled the valley of the River Tauber since 400 AD. Their conversion to Christianity began as long ago as 730, under St Boniface and a relation of his, Lioba, who founded Germany's first nunnery here in 735.

The romantic, rural market place of Tauberbischofsheim, with the town hall and half-timbered buildings

The names of two of the churches act as a reminder of the two saints. From 1237 to 1803 the town belonged to the See of Mainz, before being transferred to Baden in 1806. In 1939 it still only had 3,609 inhabitants, but the arrival of industry and the integration of six surrounding parishes has now brought that figure up to about 13,000. It is the county town of Main-Tauber County and thus home to the usual administrative authorities, but this does not deprive it of its image as a „hospital little country town."

Municipal Culture and Tourist Office: *Rathaus (Town Hall), Marktplatz 8, 97941 Tauberbischofsheim, Tel. 09341/803-13, Fax 803-89, Internet: http://www.tauberbischofsheim.de, e-mail: Info@tauberbischofsheim.de*
Tourist information in the town hall: *Easter-Oct., Mon.-Thurs. 8 am-6 pm, Fr. 8 am-12 noon, 2 pm-6 pm, Sat., Sun., and public holidays 10 am to 3 pm; Nov. to March Mo.-Thurs. 8 am-12.30 pm + 1.30 pm-4.30 pm, Fr. 8 am-12 noon.*
Kurmainzisches Schloss (manor-house) with „Türmer's Tower", now the Tauber-Franconian Rural Museum, *open from Easter to October every day (except Mondays) from 2.30 to 4.30 pm, on Sundays and public holidays also from 10 am to 12 noon.*
Conducted tours through the historic town centre, *lasting about 1½ hours, DM 50.00 for any size of group up to 40 persons.*

Tauberbischofsheim rose to fame through the most famous fencing club in the world, with Emil Beck as its trainer and „medal-making machine“. His school of fencing is now recognised as the State and Federal Competitive Centre, which even includes its own boarding school, and as the training base for Olympic competitors. In addition to many other leisure facilities in the town, the fencing club also offers amateurs an opportunity of training during the holidays. A walk through the old town centre gives the visitor an enduring impression of a historical past, the witnesses of which have been lovingly preserved by its inhabitants. The group of buildings around the market place include not only the neo-Gothic town hall (which houses the Tourist Information Office) but also the baroque Rehhof (1702) and three magnificent half-timbered houses. Exactly opposite this baroque building, but 100 years older, is the Alte Post, once the despatch office of the postal monopoly run by the Princes of Turn & Taxis. The old chemist's shop, the Sternapotheke, is in the same house as the that of Dr Franck, an early surgeon. Here was the birthplace of the grandfather of the romantic poet Clemens von Brentano; he later held the high rank of Conferenzrat and the aristocratic name of de la Roche. Other interesting patrician houses are Haus Rincker (1628, with the Neidkopf or Jealous Head in the gable) and, at the eastern part of the Hauptstrasse the Haus Mackert (1744, the baroque palace of wine merchant), and the Lieblerhaus (1628, with its wainscoting and depictions of Melusines). The church of St Lioba, in the south-eastern corner of the market square, belonged to the Franciscan monastery until the latter was dissolved in 1829. It was rebuilt in the baroque style in 1735.

If we now follow the Hauptstrasse in a westerly direction we come to the Faktoreihof which formed part of the Hoher Erz- und Domstift Mainz, in other words it was the workshops, yards and offices of a monastery belonging to the Bishop and Arch-Bishop of Mainz. The coat-of-arms, bearing the date 1741, hangs above the gateway. A little to one side, and to the north, is St Sebastian's chapel, a two-storey building put up in 1746,

1. Town hall; 2. Alte Post; 3. Sternapotheke; 4. Haus Mackert; 5. St Lioba's church; 6. Klosterhof; 7. Haus Rincker; 8. Rehhof; 9. Liebler Haus; 10. Armenspital; 11. St Sebastian's chapel; 12. Main Catholic church; 13. Faktoreihof; 14. Zwinger; 15. Kurmainzisches Schloss; 16. Bischemer Kröte; 17. Remains of town defences; 18. Maria-Hilf chapel; 19. Remains of former town defences; 20. St Peter's chapel; 21. Imperial Post and Telegram Office; 22. Sonnenplatzapotheke; 23. Main Evangelical church; 24. Police headquarters; 25. Town gate of 1612; 26. Monolith from the local area; 27. War memorial

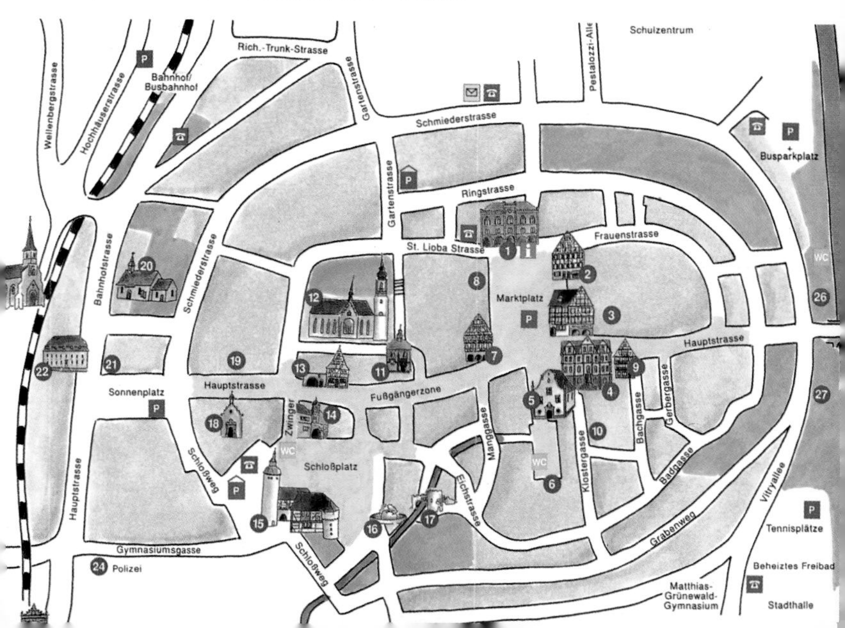

The Catholic church of St Martin, built in 1910, contains valuable old church treasures.

and the neo-Gothic church of St Martin, the interior of which contains valuable works of medieval art. Even before we reach the Maria-Hilf chapel (1700), a street called Zwinger - commemorating the „bailey“ of long-vanished fortifications - leads us downhill in the direction of the Kurmainzisches Schloss or manor house. In this street is the charming birthplace of an abbot which was built in 1595.
Parts of this manor-house had been built in 1250, but the main building dates from 1400 and was the seat of the ruling officials appointed from Mainz. Numerous coats-of-arms which include Mainz's symbol, the wheel, commemorate them. The interior of the building has housed the Tauber-Franconian Rural Museum since 1970. South of the Schlossplatz, which is dominated by the imposing „Türmer's Tower“, we find the last remains of the medieval town wall and a fountain illustrating the Bischemer Kröte - Bischemer being the term for the inhabitants of „Bischofsheim“ and Kröte - toad, or just possibly brat - being the nickname sometimes lovingly applied to them.
All over the town you will find lovingly manicured parks and gardens and nu-

The Kurmainzisches Schloss, its oriole windows decorated with coats-of-arms.

merous fountains, and on the outskirts there are innumerable wayside shrines and statues of saints; this is the centre of the so-called „Madonna Country". More than 200 kilometres of signposted hiking paths lead through vineyards and forests, but nevertheless the outlying districts of this town include the famous former beer village of Distelhausen. The sights worth seeing here include the baroque church, built in 1731 under Balthasar Neumann's supervision, the chapel of St Wolfgang (1472) on the west bank of the Tauber, and the numerous mansions of the wine merchants, more of which can also be seen in other parts of the town.

Starting from Tauberbischofsheim, it is possible to make a short excursion to Wertheim (30 kilometres), where one can visit the ruins of the castle above the River Main, the Historical Museum, and the Glass Museum. On the way we pass through Reicholzheim, and wine village steeped in tradition, and can made another short excursion of 6 kilometres to the unspoilt little town of Külsheim, famous for its fountains and its wine.

From Distelhausen, mentioned above, it is only 3 kilometres or so to Grünsfeld (parish church, town hall) and another 2 kilometres to Grünsfeldhausen (octagonal chapel, 12th century, with Roman-style frescoes).

The Kurmainzisches Schloss (from 1250 onwards) with its massive Türmer's Tower is nowadays the home of the Tauber-Franconian Rural Museum.

Lauda-Königshofen

Between Tauberbischofsheim and Bad Mergentheim, the Romantic Road runs along the B 290 main road. Barely 3 kilometres south of Distelhausen a road branches off to Gerlachsheim, which is administratively part of Lauda - Königshofen. Here we ought to look at the church (1723 - 1770), which once belonged to the former Prämonstraten Order, a missionary Order that took its name from the French abbey of Prémontré. It is a magnificent baroque building with impressive stucco work, altars, and sequences of pictures, luxuriantly decorated rococo-style pulpit, and a superb organ (1754). The stone bridge over the Grünbach forms a romantic nook, with its gigantic statues of saints. If one considers this together with the numerous monasteries and wayside shrines, one can see impressive documentary proof of the name of this stretch of countryside, the „Madonna Country“. This bridge marks the start of Wine Lore Path, along which the hiker will learn many new lessons about the centuries-old tradition of wine-making in this region. The local speciality here is not only the wine but also Grünkern, which is made from unripe wheatgerm and usually served in soup, and offered to the favoured guest in the numerous, inviting little taverns.

The main centre of this rural community is Lauda, the oldest „citadel“ of the Franconian / Allemannic Fasnacht - the semi-pagan, semi-Christian spring ceremonies before the start of Lent. However, it also possesses a town centre worth seeing, with many 17th and 18th century houses decorated with depictions of the Madonna. The town hall and the Weinbauernhaus, or vintners' house, date from the 16th century; today they house the museum of local arts and crafts with its collections of wine-growing and wine-making implements and relics of rustic life, handicrafts, railway history, and the Fasnacht tradition. Remains of the town fortifications, such as the Oberes Tor, the powder magazine tower, and the steam-engine memorial, bear witness to the importance the town enjoyed in previous centuries.

The town lies at the crossing point of the Main / Tauber / Franconian figure-of-eight cycling route, which is made up of 11 sections covering the whole area from Miltenberg to Würzburg and including Buchen and Weikersheim. The rail service is very good, so that the cyclist can reach the area easily, and this of course benefits any hiker as well who would like to cover the European figure-of-eight route in one or a number of stages, all along the

Culture and Tourist Office, *Marktplatz 1,*
97922 Lauda-Königshofen, tel. 09343/5010, fax 501100.
Sights: Museum, art gallery, churches, Oberes Tor, Pulverturm.
„Das Auge“ art gallery *open Sundays and public holidays from 10.00 am to 12.00 noon and from 2.00 to 4.00 pm, entry free.*
Museum of local arts and crafts: *April to October, Sundays and public holidays, 3.00 to 5.00 pm, and for groups also at other times by appointment with Mr Hauer, phone +09343/4517 or 501-128.*

A romantic corner on the edge of Gerlachsheim, with the Grünbach bridge and its statues of saints and towers of the monastery church.

Tauber to Wertheim or to Rothenburg ob der Tauber.
Many other opportunities offered as part of leisure facilities and the summer programme of entertainments have contributed to Lauda-Königshofen being granted the status of a „town that welcomes families".
There are more unspoilt wine-making villages: Oberlauda, Marbach, and of course Beckstein, south of Lauda. Distinguished with many medals, this pretty village

Wine lore path in the wine-making village of Beckstein.

A section of the Taubertal cycling path near Königshofen.

makes a welcoming sight nestling in the midst of the terraced vineyards which provide the local population with their livelihood. The vintners founded one of Germany's oldest wine-making co-operatives here, in the cradle of the immortal Bocksbeutel wine-bottle, as long ago as 1894, and today it is the centre for the surrounding wine-making villages. A guided tour of the cellars, followed by a wine-tasting in the Weinparadies or the vaulted St Kilian's Cellar will provide the visitor with more detailed information on the well-known quality wines and the outstanding top-quality wines of the region.

Nature has endowed this chalky region most generously in other ways as well. In the three extensive nature-protection areas in particular the nature-lover will find numerous heathland plants, including several different kinds of orchid, a rich fauna with about 600 species of butterfly and nearly 100 bird species, as well as numerous warmth-loving reptiles and amphibians.

In Königshofen itself, a number of memorable half-timbered buildings as well as the tower-like Goten and the Hohes Haus bear witness to the civic pride of earlier generations. From he we drive 6 kilometres to the next point on the Romantic Road, to the spa town of Bad Mergentheim.

The Marienstrasse in the old town centre of Lauda.

A delightful evening in the „Madonna Country“: the church tower and „Goten“ in Königshofen.

Bad Mergentheim

The town originally developed from the Court of a Franconian king at the crossing-point of major trade routes. In 1219 it was passed on as a gift from the brother Heinrich, Andreas, and Friedrich von Hohenlohe into the hands of the Deutscher Orden, an order of chivalry, which maintained a presence here.

Bad Mergentheim: Residential palace of the Deutscher Orden between 1526 and 1806.

Tourist information: Municipal Culture and Tourist Office, *Marktplatz 3, 97980 Bad Mergentheim, tel. 07931/57131, fax 57-300, Internet: http://www.bad-mergentheim.de*

Sights to see: Deutschorden Museum in the Deutschorden Palace: *open daily from 10 am - 5 pm except Mon.*
Conducted tours: Thurs., Sun. + public holidays at 3 pm. Every 2. + 4. Mon. in the month at 7.30 pm..

Schlosskirche and Münster: *are open at all times.*

Wild-life park: *open 9.00 am to 6.00 pm, ticket office closes as 5.00 pm, during winter on Saturdays and Sundays from 10.30 am until twilight.*

Palace of the Deutsch-orden: Chapter Room.

Doll's kitchen in the museum of the Deutschorden palace.

The town remained in the Order's possession until the conclusion of the Imperial Deputation in 1806, having been maintained as a residence since 1526. Their palace nowadays houses a museum reflecting the history of the Order and the town. The Meistergemächer, the suite occupied by the Masters of the Order, and the fine Chapter Room are samples of the princely way of life during the baroque, rococo, and classical periods. In addition to the collection of arms and armaments, the historical display of the Battle of Herbsthausen (1645) counts as one of the magnificent sights in this palace. Its church was built in 1730 - 36, with more than a little help from Balthasar Neumann, as the Court Chapel for the Masters of the Order, the Hoch- und Deutschmeister. The crypt became the last resting-place for many members of the Order.

A West Prussian monument is to be found in the Bläserturm or Trumpeters' Tower, from the tower room of which serenades are played by the town band in summer. The pastor's walk, decorated with Madonna's, leads to the Johanniterhof or Court of the Order of St John and to the hospice. The Knights of St John, who had competed with the Deutscher Orden for dominance over the town, built the Minster in 1300. Among its treasures is a major tomb, that of Marquardt von Eck, ruler of the order (about 1600).

The market square is almost hemmed in by fine half-timbered buildings and

baroque palaces, as well as the town hall (1564). In front of it is the octagonal Renaissance fountain with a Statue of the Deutschmeister, Wolfgang Schutzbar, also known as the „Milchling". It was he who elevated Mergentheim to the status of a Residenz in 1526.
St Mary's church, near Oberer Markt and Hans Heinrich Ehrler Platz, has been rebuilt several times in its history but still contains wall-paintings from the time of its first construction (from 1300 onwards) and a bronze epitaph of the Hochmeister Walther von Cronberg which was produced in 1539 by Hans Vischer, a master-craftsman from Nuremberg. Many other buildings along the enchanting Altstadtgassen, with their Madonna figures, statues of saints, and colourful coats-of-arms, indicate the dominance of the Order here in Herrgottsländle, God's Little Country. One particularly characteristic place is the Gothic Wolfgang's bridge across the Tauber, decorated with a statue of Nepomuk, the patron saint of bridges. Together with the crucifixion group and the church of St Wolfgang, it forms an attractive group and at the same time serves as the symbol for this local region.
In addition to all this testimony of its historical past, Bad Mergentheim offers its visitors a large number of entertainments such as a theatre, dancing, or leisure facilities in the Solymar bathing park. All this forms part of the extensive programme of the modern spa town into which Bad Mergentheim has been developing since the last century. (Almost any town with Bad in its name is a spa, where people „take the waters" and enjoy a long, healthy holiday with medical treatment called a Kur.) This was made possible by a shepherd who, in 1826, rediscovered a bitter-salt spring that had long been buried and forgotten about. Today it is the centre of attraction of the spa baths, and offers benefits to those with metabolic disorders.
The point of magnetic attraction for Kur guests and others seeking a good, healthy holiday is the Kurpark, where the Wandelhalle is particularly popular in damp weath-

View across the market square to the Twins' Houses, St John's Minster, and „Milchling's" fountain.

Stuppach parish church: Madonna (Matthias Grünewald)

er. In the summer, visitors are always fascinated by the carefully maintained and extensive rose garden.
One of the most famous pictures of the Middle Ages can be found in the side-chapel of the parish church in the adjacent village of Stuppach, some 7 kilometres south of Bad Mergentheim in the direction of Schwäbisch Hall. The Stuppach Madonna was created in 1519 by the hands of the artist Mathis Nithardt, known today by the name of Matthias Grünewald, the greatest German painter and sculptor after Dürer. This late Gothic representation of the Virgin Mary was painted in casein colours and remained almost 300 years in the possession of the Deutschmeister in Bad Mergentheim until Pastor Blumhofer acquired it for the Stuppach church in 1812 from the assets of the Order after its dissolution in 1806.

Returning to the outskirts of Bad Mergentheim, we can turn off along the B 290 main road towards the Wildpark or Wildlife park, one of Europe's leading parks in terms of the number of local species it houses. It includes a museum of local fauna with an extensive collection of insects, butterflies, and birds' eggs. Three kilometres further southwards along the B 290 brings us to a side-turning to the left which leads to Markelsheim, where wine-growing can be proved by historical documents to date back at least to 1096. This wine-growing village provides relaxation in a quiet atmosphere for anyone looking for a healthy holiday, with walks along the Wine Lore Path and enjoyable wine-tastings. The extension eastwards of this road takes us back across the River Tauber and onto the Romantic Road again, this time leading us to Weikersheim.

Weikersheim

For centuries, this was the residence of the once mighty Counts and Lords, later Princes, of Hohenlohe. The centre of the village is worth seeing; they had it adapted in the early 18th century to suit the style of their palace. The market square ends on its east side in the later Gothic parish church (1419, tombs dating from the 15th century onwards), flanked on the north and south sides by baroque houses once occupied by Court officials, and leaving space in the middle for access to the palatial complex and its main entrance.

Schloss Weikersheim, once the residence of the Princes of Hohenlohe, seen from its gardens.

Tourist information: Municipal Culture and Tourist Office,
Marktplatz 7, 97990 Weikersheim, tel. 07934/102-55, fax 102-58,
e-mail: stadt-weikersheim@t-online.de
Conducted tours: July to Oct. 5 pm at the market square.
Schlossmuseum, *opening times: 1st April to 31st October, every day, 9.00 am to 6.00 pm; November to March, every day, 10.00 am to 12.00 noon and 1.30 to 4.30 pm, tel. 07934/8364.*
Tauberland Village Museum: *Easter to 1st Nov., every day except Mondays, 10.00 am to 12.00 noon and 2.00 to 5.00 pm, tel. 07934/1209.* ***Forestry museum on the Karlsberg:*** *1st April to 15th November, Sundays, 2.00 to 5.00 pm, tel. 07934/1209.*

Schloss Weikersheim: The Rittersaal can still be seen today in the original magnificence which made it famous at the time when it was built.

Passing through a gateway (17th century) in the lower wing of the Marstall or stables heading towards the east wing, one arrives in the palace courtyard and faces its medieval keep. It is well worth looking round the completely preserved and valuable interior, most of it dating from the 18th century, such as the magnificent stucco-work in the residential rooms and in particular the Rittersaal or Knights' Hall in the south wing. It takes up two storeys of the Renaissance building (about 1600) and was regarded as the largest and most beautiful of its day. The massive grid-pattern ceiling is suspended by chains from the roof trusses, and painted with realistic hunting scenes. Valuable portraits and numerous landscapes, ornaments, and three-dimensional heads of wild animals decorate the walls. Even more overwhelming are the magnificent stucco structures around the fireplace and the entrance doorway, including a bas-relief representation of a battle with the Turks, on the short wall of the banqueting hall. Parts of this palace house an off-shoot of the Württemberg State Museum. Every year the young musicians of Musikalische Jugend Deutschlands meet here for courses, concerts, and performances of operas with international singers.
A wall through the gardens of the palace takes the visitor back through time to the baroque age, with their geometrically arranged flower-beds and paths, an orangery, and regiments of statues from antique times and from Court life in the 18th century. Between the semicircle of columns at the far end of the

garden there once stood the gilded statue of Count Carl Ludwig on a horse. As a counter-point to the courtly pomp, the Tauberland Village Museum shows the more modest implements and equipment of the simple country people, and as a mediator between the two there is the Forestry Museum in the Schlösschen or mini-palace up on the Karlsberg (1736), showing the historical development from courtiers hunting in the baroque age to our modern notions of forestry management. The Karlsberg also offers a wildlife and leisure park, and the town itself also offers plenty of leisure facilities for an active holiday.

A short excursion of only 5 kilometres south-eastwards brings us to Laudenbach; it possesses a Gothic hill chapel (15th century) which is well worth seeing.

The palace garden with its geometrical arrangement of flower-beds and paths and its numerous statues bring the baroque age back to life.

Although it was structurally rebuilt in the 17th century, because of the high quality of its interior it is well worth a visit if only on account of the artistic alabaster tomb of Field Marshal Melchior von Hatzfeld (died 1658) in the crypt.

Returning to Weikersheim and the B 19 main road, we can travel 7 kilometres further to Röttingen, the second Bavarian town (apart from Würzburg) on the Romantic Road. The section of the Tauber valley that we pass along is noticeably narrower here, and the neat vineyards gradually give way to natural landscape. Just before we reach Röttingen, in Tauberrettersheim, there is a pretty little stone bridge (1733) across the river - one more sample of Balthasar Neumann's work.

View from the entrance of the palace to the late Gothic parish church.

Two picturesque quadrant houses flank the entrance to the palace.

Röttingen

The little wine-making village of Röttingen (population: 1,800) lies at the confluence of the Rippbach and the Tauber. It was elected in 1953 to be the first ever European Town, and appeals to the visitor because of its historic town centre with picturesque carvings and graceful half-timbered buildings all around a baroque town hall that bursts with civic pride. The Sonnenuhrweg or „sun-dial route“, about 2 kilometres long, starts and finishes in this market square, passing some 20 of these now rare time instruments. The Roman-style parish church of St. Kilian also commemorates dim and distant days; its interior still preserves tombs dating from the 13th century. The fabled castle of Brattenstein has now been renovated, and during the warmer months forms the backdrop for the well-known open-air theatre. Outside the well preserved ring of defensive walls, the archaeological hiking path leads the visitor past more than 20 hill graves and the remains of rectangular fortifications dating from Celtic days. The visitor is offered a high quality of holiday with a wide range of leisure facilities and attractive parks and gardens, all in the lovely setting of forests and vineyards.

Following the road further in the direction of Rothenburg, there is a side-turning off to the left in Bieberehren (4 kilometres) signposted to Aub. This leads to Burgerroth, where there is a Roman-style chapel (13th century, with baroque interior) standing alongside a lime-tree which is a thousand years old. Aub, the larger village, was once a centre of trade along the road from Nuremberg to Augsburg. Everywhere we go we encounter testimony to this great past: parts of the town wall and its defensive towers, the fine town hall (1489) and prison, and the baroque St Mary's Column (1732), the hunting lodge of the Prince-Bishops, and the Catholic parish church (13th to 17th century). Here it is well worth going inside to see the interior, on account of the late Gothic capita and particularly the artistic crucifixion group from the hand of Tilman Riemenschneider. Some 2 kilometres further south lies Waldmannshofen, a village belonging administratively to Creglingen. Its romantic moated grange (1544) nowadays houses a fire brigade museum. The Werkhof offers week-end pottery courses, mainly outside the tourist season, for beginners and advanced students.

In Frauental, also part of Creglingen, there is an interesting nunnery church dating from the 13th century which is worth seeing. In accordance with the strict regulations of the Cistercian Order, which ruled that nuns and the laity were not allowed to be in the same church together, this building was designed on two storeys only open to the east, towards the choir. The early Gothic lower church is also worth seeing for its fine interior. Another part of the nunnery was the Fuchshof, which nowadays houses a private museum of rural crafts.

Tourist information:
Marktplatz 1, 97285 Röttingen,
Phone 09338/972855-57, Fax 205,
Internet: http://www.roettingen.de, e-mail: roettingen@t-online.de

Röttingen: Market square and town hall ▲

▼ On the „sundial route“

▲ Sundial in the Old Town

Defensive tower and church tower ▼

Creglingen

Despite the fact that 12 neighbouring villages have been administratively integrated into it, this township's population has still remained below 5,000, and they are distributed across 117 square kilometres of countryside. Nevertheless, they offer a large number of hiking and cycling routes between one village and the next which are also connected to the network of cycling routes between Würzburg, Rothenburg, and Wertheim. Theye can also be used by people in wheelchairs.

This small town became famous for the most beautiful of all Tilman Riemenschneider's carvings, which is to be found in the Herrgottskirche 2 kilometres to the south in Herrgottstal. This church was built at the command of the lords of Hohenlohe-Brauneck in 1386 - 89, after a peasant, as legend relates, had found the Host here while he was ploughing. In about 1500 their lordships decorated it with major works of art including the Altar to the Virgin Mary (1510) by Riemenschneider, already mentioned. After the church had become evangelical in 1530, the altar was closed and garlanded with wreathes. It fell into oblivion, and remained unchanged for more than three centuries until it was re-opened in 1832. This masterpiece is 11 metres high and the shrine is made of reddish pinewood with the figures in light-coloured lindenwood. It impresses the onlooker with of the splendid flow of the folds in the garments and the magnificent hair decoration, the delicately sculptured hands and the moving faces. There are more major works of art in this Herrgottskirche: the impressive crucifix, possibly created by Veit Stoss, the altar in the Choir which is believed to come from the school of the famous Veit Stoss, and fine paintings possibly by Michael Wolgemut, Albrecht Dürer's teacher.

A pilgrimage route ran from the Herrgottskirche to the Ulrichskapelle, some 3 kilometres away in Standorf. Its founder, Konrad von Hohenlohe, had it built in the 13th century in the late Roman style, and in the shape of a regular octagon.

The museum of thimbles must be unique in the world. It has been opened opposite the Herrgottskirche and shows striking thimbles from all over the world, and from Roman times to the present day. Half way between Creglingen and Rothenburg (17 kilometres), near Tauberscheckenbach, archaeologists have discovered some 1½ kilometres of the earthworks; these once surrounded a Celtic settlement that must have stood here at about the time of Christ's birth. Part of the masonry wall along the main fortification line has been restored; it consisted of layers of stones, interrupted at short intervals for greater stability by vertical wooden posts. The homestead in the interior of these fortifications takes its name of Burgstall from the fortifications themselves. A flax-breaking museum here commemorates the laborious methods by which flax used to be worked into linen cloth.

Upper Tauber Valley Tourist Information Centre:
97993 Creglingen, tel. 07933/631, fax also 631,
Internet: http://www.creglingen.de, e-mail: info@creglingen.de
Opening times of the Herrgottskirche: *April to October, every day from 9.00 am to 5.00 pm, at other times please enquire by phoning 07933/508.*
Thimble museum: *1st April to 31st October, 9.00 am to 6.00 pm; November to March, every day, 1.00 to 4.00 pm, tel. 07933 / 370.*

▲ Creglingen: Lindleinturm ▲ Octagonal chapel in Standorf ▲ „Kirchenstaffel“

▲ Herrgottskirche:
The Altar of the Virgin Mary

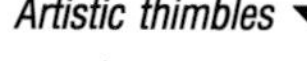

Artistic thimbles ▼ ▼ Self portrait of T. Riemenschneider

Rothenburg ob der Tauber

Shortly before the road climbs up out of the valley of the River Tauber and onto the plain on which the small but world-famous town of Rothenburg ob der Tauber stands, we will pause for a while in the outlying village of Detwang. Older than Rothenburg, it is well known for its charming Roman-style church (about 1170, renovated in Gothic times) with its magnificent cross and altar produced by Tilman Riemenschneider (1460-1531). Not far away is a tower-like house, the Töpplerschlösschen or „Töppler's little castle“ (1388) - once the summer residence of Rothenburg's most famous mayor, and nowadays open to the public. Above the valley, however, at the point where the Romantic Road and the Castles Road intersect, towers the incomparable silhouette of the former Imperial City. Reduced to poverty and insignificance mainly by the Thirty Years War,

The market square with the Renaissance town hall. As an extension, to its left, the Gothic town hall with its slender tower.

Tourist information: Culture and Tourist Office, *Marktplatz 2 (Ratsherrntrinkstube), 91541 Rothenburg ob der Tauber, tel. 09861/404-92, fax 86807*
Jakobskirche, *Easter to October, 09.00 am to 5.30 pm, otherwise 10.00 am to 12.00 noon and 2.00 to 4.00 pm.*
Reichstadtmuseum: *April to October, 10.00 am to 5.00 pm; November to March, 1.00 to 4.00 pm.*
Dolls and toys museum: *March to December, 9.30 am to 6.00 pm, January and February 11.00 am to 5.00 pm.*
Criminology museum: *April to October, 9.30 to 6.00 pm; November to February, 2 to 4 pm; during Christmas Market (until 6th January), and in March, 10 am to 4 pm.*

the medieval appearance of the old Franconian town, complete with its encircling wall and defensive towers, remained unchanged for centuries.
Anyone who intends to explore Rothenburg properly needs days for it. For visitors who are only here for a short stay, we recommend a tour round the most important sights in the old town centre, starting at the Marktplatz; without viewing any interiors, this will take about 2 hours. The western side of the historic square is formed by the soaring gable of the Ratsherrntrinkstube or Councillors' drinking-room (1446), with a sundial and the town clock (1683). The small windows at the side open every hour on the hour to show the main figures involved in the Meistertrunk; according to tradition, this was a magic potion which the fighting men of the town drank in 1631 before storming out against a besieging army and thus saved the town from destruction. The south side is formed by the magnificent Rathaus, or town hall, with its Renaissance building (1572 - 78, arcades added 1681) turned towards the square. The Gothic western part of the building with the slender clock-towers, which survived the great fire of 1501 unscathed, still today serves as a reminder of the old town hall. In this building the Kaisersaal or Imperial Hall, the historical vaults, and the dungeons are all well worth visiting. There is an incomparable architectural group on the tower side of the town hall, consisting of the attractive fountain called either St George's or the Herterichsbrunnen (1608), with the half-timbered gable wall of the former Fleisch- und Tanzhaus, a butchers' guild hall also used for dancing

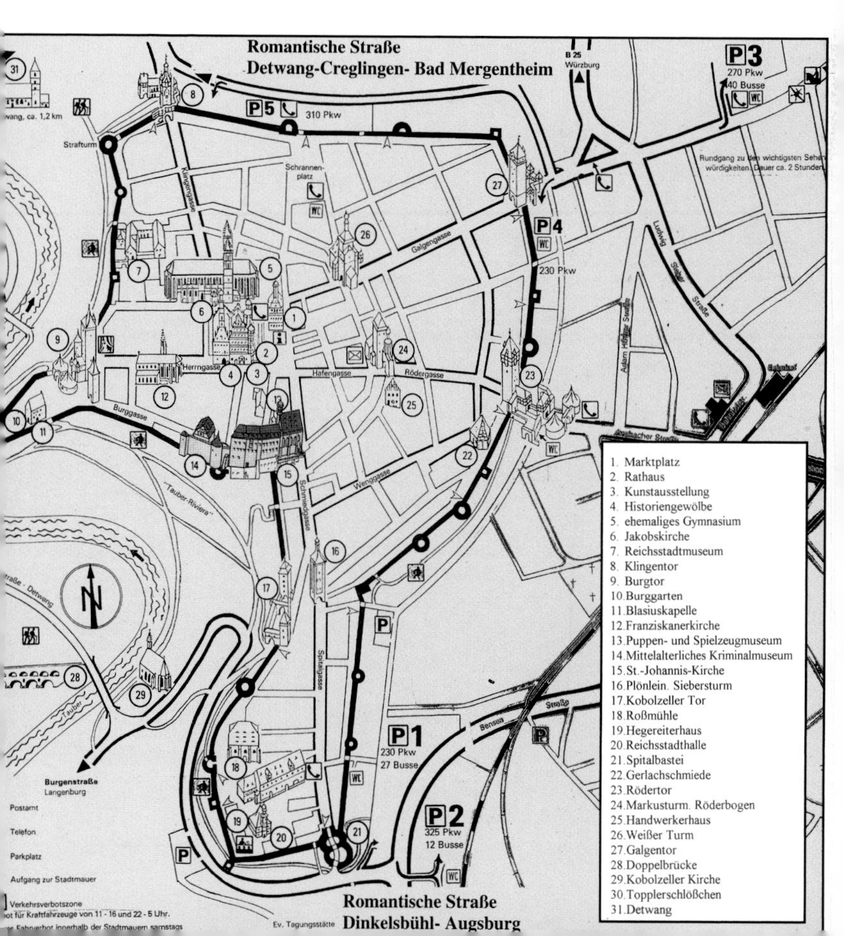

and revelry (13th century), and the Jagstheimerhaus (1488), once the home of a wealthy merchant and now housing a traditional pharmacy, the Marienapotheke. With its picturesque oriole window above a statue of a saint, the building is one of the finest patrician houses in Rothenburg.
There is an open courtyard between the town hall buildings which gives us access to the town's principal church, the Gothic Jakobskirche (1311-1484). The long time taken to build the church is reflected in the difference in design between the cupolas on the towers. On its north side there is a harmonious Renaissance building, the former Gymnasium or Grammar School. In the interior of the Jakobskirche, with its innumerable

Jakobskirche: The Altar of the Holy Blood by the famous wood-carver Tilman Riemenschneider, with the Last Supper as its centrepiece.

wealth of works of art, two items are particularly worth looking it: the brilliantly colourful, gilded High Altar, with magnificent painted panels by Friedrich Herlin (1466), and beneath it a representation of the market square of Rothenburg at that time, and the Altar of the Holy Blood on the western altar steps. This is one of the most impressive works of the carver Riemenschneider, and depicts the Last Supper. The Louis of Toulouse altar came from the hands of the same artist. In addition to these, the church possesses valuable statues, epitaphs, and glass paintings, some of which (at the end of the Choir) date from the 14th century.
Under the West Front, the Klingengasse leads away to the north, and we follow it past the picturesque Feuerleinserker (an oriole window, about 1600) and then turn left into the courtyard of the former Dominican cloister (13th century), the historical rooms of which nowadays house the Reichstadtmuseum, the museum depicting the town's history as an Imperial City. A number of living rooms, bedrooms, stores, and suchlike have been preserved, including the herbal and monastery kitchen (about 1300), which must now be the oldest kitchen in Germany. Then there is the famous cycle of pictures depicting the „Rothenburg Passion“ (1494, Martinus Schwarz), in the early Gothic crossing, and numerous exhibits reflecting everyday life for the earliest citizens, and the Prince-Elector's wine tankard of 1616, which held 3¼ litres of wine - nearly a US gallon - and was handed round when visitors were being welcomed.
The Klingengasse leads on towards the Klingenturm (13th century), a tower and barbican (1500) belonging to St Wolfgang's church, which had no tower of its own. This church was the place of worship of the country people from the district, particularly shepherds, and at the same time formed part of the defences

A romantic section of the northern town wall with the Klingenturm, where the walkway is roofed over and accessible to visitors.

for the townspeople. Accordingly, in the interior there is not only a fine altar but also defensive buildings; the steps up to the outer gateway tower (now called the Schäfertanz-Kabinett, or shepherds' dancing-room) provide access to the fortifications of the north wall, which is then connected to the gun emplacements and casemates built in below the floor of the church. From the inside the barbican, a footpath leads us outside the town walls across the Tauber valley to the Burggarten or castle garden, where once the old castles, the Grafenburg (about 1000) and the Reichsburg (12th century) used to stand until they were both destroyed in an earthquake in 1356. However, it is more than worthwhile to visit the gardens on account of the view out over the valley and along the town wall to the south, and to see St Blasius' chapel, built in 1400 out of material salvaged from the Reichsburg. We leave it through the gateway with the coats-of-arms, the Burgtor (14th century), and enter the Herrngasse, lined on either side by magnificent patrician houses with romantic internal courtyards (Nos. 18, 15, 13, and 11). On the right we can see the Franciscan church (about 1300), which contains not only the painted rood screen but also artistic epitaphs and the Altar of St Francis (Tilman Riemenschneider). Passing a fine fountain, the Herrnbrunnen, we reach the picturesque Hofbronnengasse opposite the town hall, where we can visit a dolls and toys museum. At the beginning of the next parallel street, the Schmiedgasse, we are greeted by the attractive Renaissance façade of the Baumeisterhaus, with its depiction of the Seven Virtues and the Seven Deadly Sins. The internal courtyard is particularly beautiful; it is used nowadays as a café. On the right of the Baumeisterhaus is the former home of Mayor Toppler (about 1400, gable added in the 17th century).

The way Rothenburg's old town developed can be seen particularly clearly in

View across the Tauber valley of the silhouette of the old Imperial City, with the striking tower of the town hall. In the foreground is the historic „double bridge".

View along the Herrngasse, which in past centuries was the favourite residential area for wealthy families, and also a horse-market. The fountain in the foreground is the Herrnbrunnen.

the Schmiedgasse. The hinges of the old south gate of the town (12th century) can still be seen today on the Johanniskirche, and on the left the street called Alter Stadtgraben marks the former line of the town wall. On the right, in the building which once housed the Order of St John, is the well-stocked Medieval Criminology Museum, the most important museum in Germany for forensic science. A few metres further southwards, from Plönlein, we can see two town gates at once which were built when the town was extended in 1204; the defensive gate of the Kobolzeller Tor with its barbican leading down into the valley where, far below it, the double bridge has spanned the Tauber since 1330; and the Siebersturm at the end of the Schmiedgasse which became superfluous when the town was extended for the second time in the 14th century and it then formed the entrance to the new suburb, the Spitalviertel.

Starting from the Siebersturm we keep over to the right and follow the walkway of the town walls. Passing the old horse-driven mill, the Rossmühle (built in 1516), and a tithe barn, the Zehntscheuer, we reach the internal courtyard of the Spital or infirmary, in the centre of which stands the attractive Hegereiterhaus. The most noteworthy of the buildings surrounding this courtyard are the Spi-

CITY MUSEUM

Rothenburg ob der Tauber

Convent  Culture

The City Museum was formerly a Dominican convent. Along with the town hall and the Church of St. Jacob it is one of the most important architectural monuments in the City of Rothenburg. Although the convent suffered a bitter loss when the church was demolished in 1812, the other convent buildings are of supreme importance in terms of cultural history. The first nuns came from Würzburg to enter into the noble religious foundation in 1528, the last died in 1554. Today, the buildings house the city's collections of art and historical artifacts, which, with works such as the "Rothenburg Passion", the sculptures of the Church of St. Jacob, the *"Meistertrunkhumpen"*, and an important collection of Judaica, has the rank of a regional museum. The 13th century convent kitchen and furniture, weapons, and household articles round out the extensive cultural and historical collections. Open: Apr.-Oct.: 9:30 am - 5:30 pm; Nov.-Mar.: 1:00 - 4:00 pm. Information: Klosterhof 5, D-91541 Rothenburg, Germany, Phone: +49 9861/939043.

1000 Jahre Rechtsgeschichte unter einem Dach

This, the most important legal museum in Germany, offers a broad insight into the legal happenings, laws and punishments of the past 1000 years. The presentations cover the development of legislation up through the 19th century. The course of medieval criminal trials, torture instruments and devices for administering corporal and capital punishment is shown. The collection also includes devices, some of them very funny to the casual observer, for administering degrading punishments, such as neck collars for quarrelsome women, masks of shame or stocks. Legal history is inseparable from documents and the seals that make them legally binding. Numerous documents bear witness to the trouble that went into their design. A great deal of space is also taken up by copperplates and woodcuts of sensational criminal cases. Police regulations demonstrate how the power of the government extended to the most intimate sphere of life in the form of clothing, marriage, and baptismal regulations. The collection of coins and medallions commemorating legislation or famous court cases, and exhibits dealing with legal symbolism, slang expressions oritinating in law, and cartoons lambasting judical and administrative authorities are also worthy of mention.

Open: April-October: 9:30 AM - 6:00 PM; Nov., Jan., Feb. 2:00 - 4:00 PM; Dec., Mar. 10:00 AM - 4:00 PM. Information: Burggasse 3-5, D-91541 Rothenburg o.d.T., Germany. Phone +49 9861/5359; Fax +49 9861/8258; http//www/Info@Kriminalmuseum Rothenburg.de; AOL: Krimmus@aol.com

A famous scene for painters: from „Plönlein" with the Siebersturm (left) and the Kobolzeller Tor, defending the approach up from the Tauber valley with its massive barbican.

Gerlachschmiede with the town wall and the Rödertor.

talkirche, or hospice chapel (with sculptures and epitaphs dating from the 14th and 15th centuries), the Spitalturm tower (1574 - 78) with its fine interior, the lower half-timbered building containing cellars, a bake-house, a well-house, and a quarantine house for plague victims. We now leave the courtyard and go up the Spitalgasse, the southern end of which is formed by another barbican, the Spitalbastei, the youngest (1537-42 and 1586) and most massive of Rothenburg's bastions. Here we can climb up onto the walkway of the town walls and follow it northwards, to the end of the Spitalviertel, and then eastwards. Amongst the interesting little houses below us there is one particularly attractive one, the Gerlachschmiede, once a smithy, which we reach just before coming to the Rödertor, a barbican which we can enter and look at. On the way, which leads us back towards the town centre, we can cast a glance at a particularly picturesque group of buildings: the Röderbogen archway with its ridge turrets, the massive tower of St Mark's flanked by magnificent patrician houses, and, in the foreground, the fine Röderbrunnen fountain. Anyone who feels like visiting a museum can be recommended to try the Old Rothenburg Handwerkerhaus, a craftsman's house in Alter Stadtgraben (a side-turning near the Röderbogen) which has remained almost unchanged since it was built in the 13th century. Its living rooms and workshops are furnished in the style of past centuries. Behind the Röderbogen, on its right, the old town prison Büttelhaus leans up against St Mark's church. If we proceed straight ahead we take the shortest route back to the Marktplatz, or if we turn off to the right we can pass through Milchmarkt, the milk-market, and Kappelenplatz, to reach the Weisser Turm (white tower) with its Judentanzhaus (Jews' dancing hall). Particularly when seen from this vantage-point in the Galgengasse, this building with its attractive half-timbered oriole windows presents a very fine sight. The Weisser Turm likewise fulfilled its role as a town gate for only a few years before being superseded by the Galgentor (Gallows Gate!) in the present town wall. By going along the Georgengasse we come back to the Marktplatz, where our tour started. In addition to these many sights, from Easter of each year onwards there are historical performances of the Schäfertanz (shepherds' dance) and the Hans Sachs festival, and from Whitsun onwards the famous Meistertrunk draws numerous visitors to the town.

The Georgengasse and the Weisser Turm

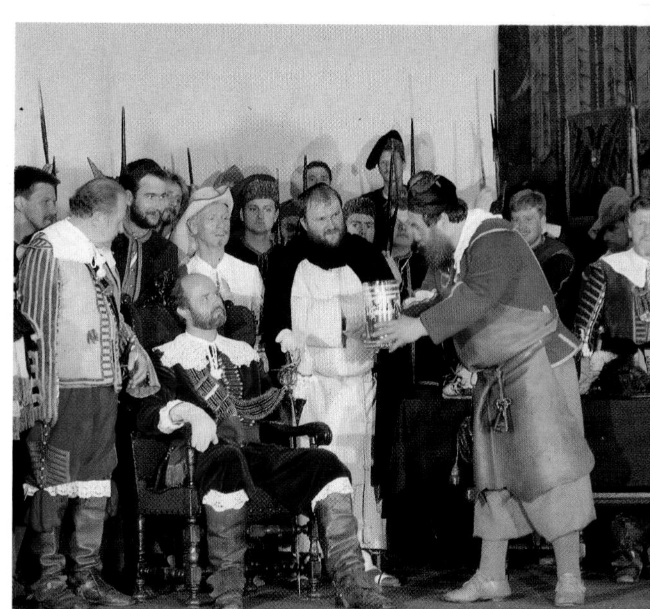

Historical festival of the „Meistertrunk“: the cellar-master hands Tilly the goblet holding the drink of welcome.

9 Schillingsfürst

We initially leave Rothenburg and travel 10 kilometres southwards along the B 25 main road, and turn off to the left in Insingen. A further 7 kilometres brings us to the small town of Schillingsfürst, nestling beneath the imposing baroque mansion of the Princes of Hohenlohe-Schillingsfürst. It boasts 70 rooms, lit by 365 windows. Rich stucco work, artistic ceiling paintings and tapestries, lovingly selected furniture, fine porcelain and valuable portraits bring the 18th and 19th centuries back to life. The study of Chancellor Chlodwig, a successor of Bismarck as Chancellor of the German Empire, still contains its original furniture dating from around 1900. The palace invites the visitor to see a museum with a priceless interior and loving details.

There had already been a massive castle at this exposed position in the Year 1000, but this was destroyed on a number of occasions. The present com-

Schillingsfürst, the town and palace on the Frankenhöhe, which at this point represents the European watershed between the Rhine and the Danube.

Tourist information: Schillingsfürst Municipal Tourist Office,
Anton Roth Weg 9, 91583 Schillingsfürst, tel. 09868/800, fax 986233,
Internet: http://www.schillingsfuerst.de, e-mail: howo@rothenburg.netsurf.de
Bavarian Falconry Centre and Palace Museum:
Opening times: all year round, with falcon shows from 1st March to 31st October. Castle tours: 10.15 am, 12.00 noon, 2 pm, 4 pm. Falcon shows 11 am and 3 pm. May to Sept. also 5 pm. Tel. 09868/6941.
***Brunnenhausmuseum:** tours by prior arrangement, tel 09868/800.*

Schloss Schillingsfürst: Red Saloon

Tapestry Saloon

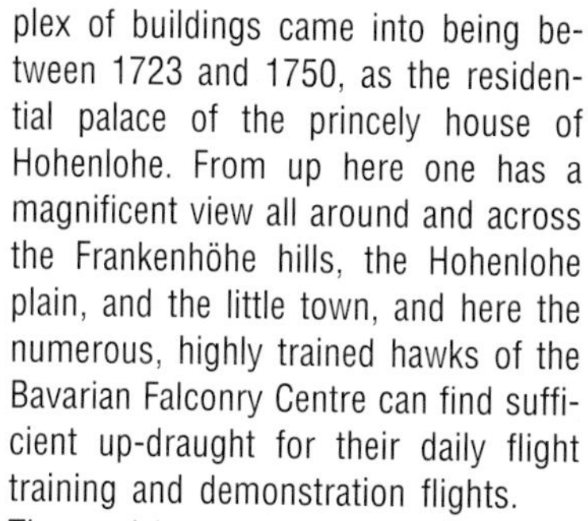

plex of buildings came into being between 1723 and 1750, as the residential palace of the princely house of Hohenlohe. From up here one has a magnificent view all around and across the Frankenhöhe hills, the Hohenlohe plain, and the little town, and here the numerous, highly trained hawks of the Bavarian Falconry Centre can find sufficient up-draught for their daily flight training and demonstration flights.
The road leading downwards from the palace comes to a water-tower that looks more like a lighthouse. From there we follow the signposts to the Brunnenhausmuseum, and after 1 kilometre come to a solitary house overshadowed by an old water-tower. The pumping machinery from which the museum takes its name is unique, consisting of an „ox's treadmill“ in which the sloping wooden turntable was rotated by the animal's walking action and brought the water up into the water-tower by means of a pump. From there it flowed through wooden pipes, called „Deicheln", to the palace. The adjoining museum of local arts and crafts is also worth seeing.
At Oberwörnitz (5 kilometres) we come back onto the B 25 main road and travel another 13 kilometres southwards to the town of Feuchtwangen.

Flight demonstrations by hawks commemorate the aristocratic hunting methods of the Middle Ages.

10 Feuchtwangen

The town originally developed around a Benedictine monastery founded in the 8th century. From some time in the 12th century until 1376 it was a Free Imperial City, but was then ceded to the Counts of Brandenburg-Ansbach, and since 1806 has belonged to Bavaria. Its population is now something over 10,000.

The Marktplatz (Market square) presents a rare spectacle of harmony and completeness which has earned it the name of „Franconia's Festival Hall". Proud patrician houses, most of them nowadays devoted to the hotel and catering trade, and the magnificent Altes Rathaus line the edges of the long, narrow Platz. Its northern end is formed by the Gothic monastery church (13th/14th century), which replaced the former Roman-style monastery church of St Salvator. It had originally belonged to

Feuchtwangen: View across the market square with the baroque fountain and the former town hall, with the Gothic monastery church in the background.

Tourist information: Municipal Culture and Tourist Office,
Marktplatz 1, 91555 Feuchtwangen, tel. 09852/90444, fax 904260.
Franconian museum and singers' museum:
opening times: every day except Mondays and Tuesday 10 am to 12 noon and 2 to 5 pm in March, November, and December, 10 am to 12 noon and 2 to 6 pm from April to October, close in January and February.
Craftsmen's rooms: *on request (telephone 09852/90444).*
Churches: *on request (telephone 09852/90444).*

Feuchtwangen: Scene from the Crossing Play (in the background is the Roman-style crossing of the former Benedictine monastery).

the Benedictine monastery mentioned above, but was converted in 1150 to a Chorherrenstift, a church with a choir under the patronage of the local aristocracy. It has served since 1623 as the main Evangelical-Lutheran church of Feuchtwangen. Inside, the High Altar, painted in 1483 by Michael Wolgemut, the master who taught Dürer, the carvings on the Choir stool (about 1500), and the tomb of the monastery's patron Lucas Freyer (1523) deserve particular attention.

On the south side of the monastery church is the late-Roman style crossing, dating right back to the time of the Benedictine monastery. In the upper storey, above the west wing, there are six original workshops in the „Craftsmen's rooms": a sugar-baker, a dyer, a pewter-caster, a potter, a cobbler, and a weaver. Every year, during the summer months, the well-known Crossing Plays take place, using the inner courtyard as an open-air theatre. Parallel to the monastery church, and along its rear wall, stands the parish church of St John, which started life as the baptismal chapel of the former royal Court. The present-day building dates from about 1400. Behind it, and parallel to the two large churches, a chapel to St Peter and St Paul (1333/34) was originally built in the churchyard and was converted in 1565 by the townspeople into a grain warehouse. Today it serves as a roomy municipal hall.

We will now return to the Marktplatz. The baroque fountain on the south side, the Röhrenbrunnen (1727), is decorated not only with the figure on the column but also by a colourful genealogy illustrated with coats-of-arms. The Museumsgasse starts just alongside the fountain, and is full of gabled houses which are either historically genuine or authentically restored. Almost at the far end of the street, a wooden pump and a stone money-counter mark the Franconian Museum, housed in a building dating from 1789. Inside, room-settings showing townspeople's lives from the baroque to the Art Nouveau ages can be seen, and in particular a very fine collection of faience ware. The modern extension to the museum building occupies the earlier site of a synagogue, built in 1833 and destroyed in the wave of racial hatred in 1938. The fountain opposite is dedicated to the medieval bard, Walther von der Vogelweide (about 1200) and his poetry, and the nearby Franconian Singers' Museum to the history of the Franconian Singers' Association (since 1989).

A further 12 kilometres southwards along the B 25, which here is both the Romantic Road and the Franconian Wine Road, take us to the little town of Dinkelsbühl.

Dinkelsbühl

The original settlement arose as the Court of a Frankish king, and was fortified before the start of our millennium as a place of refuge on the trading routes, from the Baltic to Italy and from Worms to Prague, that intersected here.

It was at this cross-roads that the late Gothic St George's church arose (1448 - 99), which strikes the eye because of its false proportions: the nave on the one hand is too high and the tower on other hand, despite being 62 metres tall, still

Dinkelsbühl: View of the west tower of St George's church and the neighbouring row of houses in Dr Martin Luther Strasse.

__Tourist information: Municipal Tourist Office,__ Marktplatz, 91550 Dinkelsbühl, tel. 09851/90240, fax 90279, Internet: http://www.dinkelsbuehl.de, e-mail: tourismus@dinkelsbuehl.btl.de

Opening times:

__St George's Minster:__ every day, 9 am to 12 noon and 2 to 6 pm.

__Historical museum:__ March to Nov., 9.30 am to 12 noon and 1 to 5; Dec. to Feb., 10 am to 12 noon and 2 to 4 pm; every day except Mon. in both cases.

__„3-Dimension" museum:__ April to Oct., every day, 10 am to 6 pm; Nov., Dec., Jan., Feb., March, Sat. and Sun., 11 am to 4 pm, but from 26th December to 6th January every day from 11 am to 4 pm.

seems very low. This is due to the fact that the tower we see today was built about 1225 for the earlier church on this site, a smaller one in the Roman style. A Gothic church tower was planned for the north flank, but for economic reasons only the ground floor, which now serves as a vestry, was built. On the other hand, the nave was built by the master builders of churches, Nikolaus Eseler father and son, in only 51 years and all as one complete unit, so that St George's is now regarded as the most beautiful church of its type in southern Germany.

Not only the outside wall but also the interior is designed to be harmonious without being monotonous. The six side-altars date from the time when the church was completed or, as in the case of the High Altar, shrine tableaux and figures were produced at the time and later set in a neo-Gothic housing. Another remarkable feature is the Sacrament House, 12 metres high, in which the Holy of Holies is preserved as perhaps nowhere else in Germany. In 1500 or shortly after, the Huster Epitaph was created

The central nave and choir of the late Gothic St George's church.

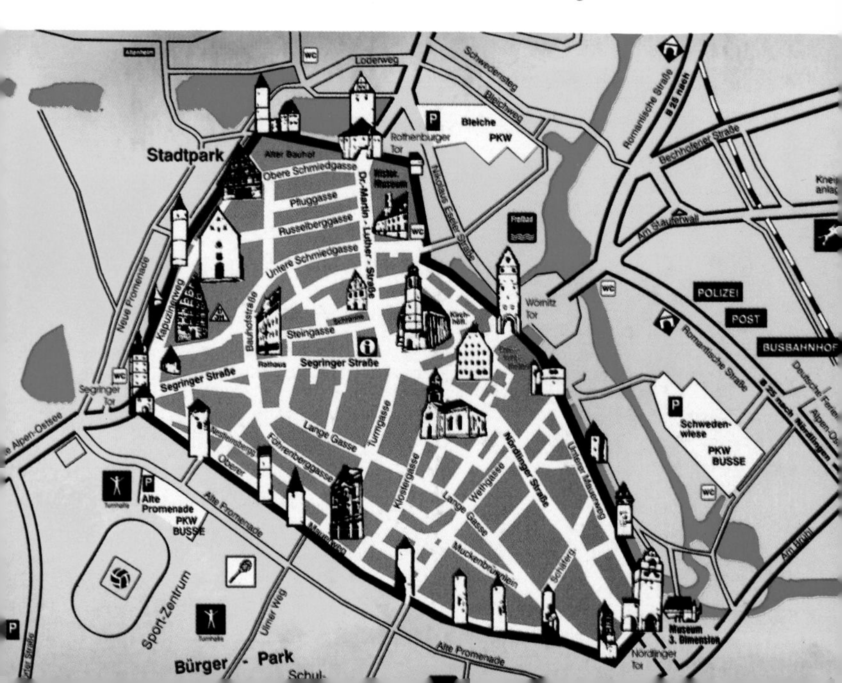

as one of the most important tombs of all, with a representation of the large family in the predella. However, the oldest work of art here is a Vespers picture (14th century, under the gallery) showing the plaintive Virgin Mary holding the child-like Christ on her arm.
One of the monuments on the south side of the church is dedicated to the Dinkelsbühl theologian and young people's writer Christoph von Schmid, who immortalised the text of the Christmas carol „Ihr Kinderlein, kommet". Opposite the Roman-style tower gateway begins the Segringer Strasse, on the left-hand side of which the eye is caught by the Hezelhaus with its fine half-timbered façade and projecting gable wall. The dreamy inner courtyard deserves particular attention, as it takes the visitor straight back to the Middle Ages. On the right-hand side of the Segringer Strasse, a particularly harmonious row of houses starts with the turreted Ratstrinkstube (the town councillor's drinking-room, about 1600), the other outstanding examples being the richly decorat-

▲ ***The Deutsches Haus proudly presents its magnificent half-timbered gable wall.***

The romantic inner courtyard of the Hezelhaus *Autumn around the dreamy Gaulweiher.*

ed, half-timbered Deutsches Haus and the powerful gable façade of the Schranne. This is where Dr Martin Luther Strasse starts, leading to the northern town gate, the Rothenburger Tor. Just before we reach that we will see the complex of buildings of the Spital, an infirmary endowed in 1280 (the present-day buildings date from the 15th and 16th centuries). Today they include an old-people's home and a museum of local arts and crafts. The choir and the vestry of the Spitalkirche still date from the 14th century.

There is one particularly picturesque view of the Rothenburger Tor (about 1390), covered with its colourful coats-of-arms, and its outbuildings, from the outside of the Spitalkirche out across the Gaulweiher pond. We therefore recommend continuing the tour by passing to the left outside the town walls. And the end of the pond is another tower, the Faulturm, with romantic outbuildings. The ponds around the town accommodate another speciality of Dinkelsbühl: carp. These fish are responsible for the nickname of Blausieder, „blue-boilers", long given to the inhabitants of Dinkelsbühl.

A walk through the neatly tended park leads past the massive Grüner Turm to the Segringer Turm, and then on past no fewer than eight more defensive towers to the

▲ *Dinkelsbühl children's band.*

„Children's story" festival. ▶

◀ *Traditional rustic dress.*

Army camp. ▼

Nördlinger Tor. Before returning at this point into the old town centre, we can stay outside the town a little to the east in order to look across the Wörnitz to this side of the fortifications. The particularly pleasing features are the Bäuerlinsturm, with its half-timbered superstructure and sloping roof, with St George's church and the higgledy-piggledy roofs of the old town in the background. The massive Stadtmühle, or town mill, alongside the Nördlinger Tor, looks just as much like part of the defences as do the walls themselves. It was built in 1378, after the Emperor Karl IV had granted the town the privilege of operating two mills. As it lay outside the town walls it was fitted out with a fortified wall, with a walkway, arrow-slits, and circular defensive turrets. The gable on the street side is the only part that was not built until about 1600.

We can now go through the Nördlinger Tor (14th century, stepped gable about 1600) and re-enter the town centre. Just before we reach the main church we encounter a baroque fountain and the Evangelical church of St Paul (1840), the successor to the Carmelite church. From the Klostergasse we can go and see the interior courtyard of the monastery, which was founded in 1290. Round-arched arcades shield priceless old 16th-century gravestones from the worst of the weather. Two illustrations commemorate the growers of durum wheat („Dinkel") who, according to legend, founded the settlement of Dinkelsbühl. At the Nördlinger Strasse the Klostergasse opens out into the Ledermarkt with its historic gabled houses. It is dominated by the massive structure of the Altes Rathaus, which was built as long ago as 1361 as the home of a wealthy citizen. It was made over to the town in the 16th century, which after making the necessary extensions used it for its council meetings until 1855. It now houses the historical basis of the Kinderzeche historic festival, one of the oldest and most famous of its kind in Germany. It is a play that has been enacted in July every year since 1897 to depict the legendary rescue of the town in 1632 through the beseeching of the chil-

Mühlgraben and the town wall, with the Bäuerlinsturm.

dren of the town. Another point worth attention is the entrance hall of the Altes Rathaus with its heavy wood ceiling and spiral staircase (1548).

The focal point of the Altrathausplatz is the Löwenbrunnen, a fountain featuring a lion holding a coat-of-arms. Neatly maintained gabled houses form, together with the Wörnitztor, a picturesque backdrop for the fountain and for the children's play, the second part of which is always given here.

Before travelling all 13 kilometres southwards along the B 25 main road to Wallerstein, we can turn off to the left after 8 kilometres, in Fremdingen, and visit Hochaltingen (with its church of St Mary of the Pilgrimage) and then travel on to Oettingen, a baroque town with a stately home and town hall (1431). Before returning to the Romantic Road, it is worthwhile visiting the Minorite monastery in Maihingen.

Wallerstein

A small market town with a population of 3,000, its slender Dreifaltigkeitssäule, a column dedicated the Holy Trinity and also called the Pestsäule, or „plague column", stands immediately behind the parish church (1613) as if in the middle the main motor road and greets the visitor from afar. This obelisk stands on a plinth bearing Latin inscriptions, and rises upwards between the three saints entrusted with keeping plague away: St Rochus, St Sebastian, and St Anthony of Padua, to the golden halo which, together with angels and clouds, symbolises the Christian Heaven. At its peak, God the Father and God the Son sit in majesty, forming the Trinity together with the Holy Ghost. At their feet sits Mary the Mother of God as advocate of the oppressed, and is crowned Queen of Heaven. The column was built in 1722-25 as a copy of a Viennese predecessor. Behind it and to the left, a road leads up to the Altes Schloss, the buildings of which have been preserved to the present day, grouped around a rough cliff in the middle of a small park. On the left, behind a prestigious gateway (1582), an administrative building is integrated into the outer ring of workshops and similar buildings. It is still worth climbing to the top of the central cliff just to enjoy the magnificent all-round view. The medieval castle of the Staufer monarchs (1188) passed into the possession of the Counts of Oettingen in 1261, and was later besieged and stormed by the Swedes. Simpler new buildings arose further down, in the village, on the edge of the Court garden, to replace it, and these were brought together into a three-wing building early in the 19th century. In the right-hand wing, containing a series of art galleries, there is also the Chapel of St Anna (1489) which houses not only remarkable statues of the saints but also an artistic carved wooden bas-relief of the Holy Family. The building itself houses a museum with an interesting collection of porcelain.

An archway through the central wing, the Welscher Bau, leads through to the extensive park. Immediately on the left is a strikingly massive three-section building, the Princes' riding school (1741-51): long, low stables, the three-storey residential building, and a high sloping roof above the central section covering the oval of the riding track. The three-wing building at the far end of the park is the Moritzschlösschen, which served at various times as the Dower House. It was built in about 1800, as were many of the other buildings in the town, such as those in the Sperlingstrasse, recognisable by the French look of their sloping roofs. Even more prestigious than the single-storey houses of the Court servants were the two-storey houses of the Court officials, who likewise helped the small town to gain in prestige, as did the similarly designed Maria Ward Institut. The Principality of Oettingen-Wallerstein lost its independence in 1806 and was integrated into Bavaria.

The B25 leads to the historic City of Nördlingen, which is only around 6 km away. A detour that is approx. six times longer, but worth every minute, leads to Baldern Castle (11th cent. fortress owned by the Princes and Counts of Oettingen since 1280; extensive collection of weapons and interesting Baroque rooms open for viewing) and Bopfingen (Town Hall from 1586 with stocks, Herlin Altar).

Markt Wallerstein Tourist information: *Weinstrasse 19, 86757 Wallerstein, tel. 09081/27600, fax 276020.*

New Castle:

Contucted tours 16th March to 31st October, every day, 10:00 am - 5:00 pm; closed on Mondays.

Fürst Wallerstein, *Schlösser & Museen, Berg 78, 86757 Wallerstein,*
Internet: http://www.fuerst wallerstein.de, e-mail: schloesser@fuerst wallerstein.de

Wallerstein: Schlosspark with St Anna's chapel . ▲

◀ In the park of the Neues Schloss.

The Red Salon with paintings from Johann Jakob Mettenleiters (1750-1825) ▼

▲ Dining room with exhibits of porcelain by renowned manu-facturers.

Plague column and parish church in Wallerstein.

Nördlingen

The area of the town was already settled in Roman and Allemanic times. „Nordlinga“ is recorded in 898 as one of the Royal courts of the Carolinian monarchs, and in 1219 it held a Whit Fair that lasted for 10 days and made it one of the most important trade fairs of Upper Germany. This brought it economic and political power, and this can still be seen in its buildings, monuments, and works of art. As a Free Imperial City (from 1215 onwards) it could afford, in the 14th century, to extended its defensive walls considerably and to incorporate the foregate, which had by then grown much larger. During the course of the Thirty Years War the town lost not only half its population but also its economic power and

The defensive walls around the old town centre of Nördlingen look as if they had been drawn by a pair of compasses, with St George's church as the centre.

Tourist information: Nördlingen Tourist Office, *Marktplatz 2, 86720 Nördlingen im Ries, tel. 09081/4380 or 84116, fax 84113, Internet: http://www. noerdlingen.de, e-mail: stadt.noerdlingen@t-online.de*

Rieskrater Museum: *open every day except Mondays, 10.00 am to 12.00 noon and 1.30 to 4.30 pm. Tel. 09081/273822-0.*

Municipal museum: *open every day except Mondays from Easter Saturday to the middle of October 1.30 to 4.30 pm. Access only as part of a guided tour. Tel. 09081/273823-0.*

St George's church: *open every day except Mondays from Eastern to 31st October, 9.30 am to 12.30 noon and 2.00 to 5.00 pm, from 1st November to Maundy Thursday 11.30 am to 12.00 noon. Tel. 09081/4035.*

Thiemig gallery: *guided tours by prior arrangement with the Tourist Office.*

Stadtmauer-Museum: *Open 1st of March to 31st Oct. from 10 am - 4:30 pm. Tel. 09081/84-120.*

importance. It was not until 1939 that the population regained the numbers it had had in 1618, just short of 9,000. Thus there was very little change here over a period of three centuries. Even the encircling walls and defensive towers have been preserved, and together with numerous other historic buildings contribute to making Nördlingen a magnetic centre for visitors from all over the world. In addition to a tour round the main sights worth seeing listed here, a walk round the outside of the town defences will be a treat for anyone interested in medieval architecture and buildings.

The starting point for any tour of the old town centre has to be the Marktplatz or market square, which contains the Tanzhaus and the Hohes Haus, both built in 15th century. The latter is a 9-storey warehouse, and the Tanzhaus possesses a magnificent half-timbered gable with three storeys, each of its three storeys protruding far out beyond the one below it. Its main purpose originally was as a market for the cloth-traders visiting the trade fair. A standing portrait of the Emperor Maximilian I, a patron of the town, decorates the otherwise plain façade facing the market square. The

1. Tanzhaus and Hohes Haus; 2. Town hall; 3. Leihhaus/Kanzlei; 4. Kürschner or Hafenhaus; 5. Klösterle; 6. Tanners' houses; 7. Holzhof; 8. Municipal museum; 9. Spitalhof; 10. Rosswette; 11. Municipal hall; 12. Winter's house; 13. Herrgottskirche or St Salvator's church; 14. Old barbican; 15. Mint; 16. Ellinger Haus; 17. Pfarrgasse; 18. St George's church; 19. New mill; 20. Kronschranne; 21. Deininger Tor; 22. Reissturm; 23. Reimlinger Tor; 24. Feilturm; 25. Former site of New Barbican; 26. Berger Tor; 27. Löwenturm; 28. Upper water tower; 29. Backofentürme; 30. Baldinger Tor; 31. Spitzturm; 32. Löpsinger Tor; 33. Railway station; 34. Post office

The magnificent Renaissance staircase of the Nördlingen town hall, with the tower of St George's church, the famous „Daniel", in the background.

Rathaus or town hall on the opposite side was also built in the 13th century as a traders' market, but has been used as the town hall since as long ago as 1382, which makes it one of the oldest in Germany. The outside Renaissance staircase with its doorway is a magnificent sample of the mason's work; it replaced a wooden access staircase at the rear of the building in 1618. Opposite is the old Leihhaus, where the Tourist Office now resides.

If we now follow the Eisengasse along the north edge to the right, and then turn off into the next narrow street to the left, we come to an open square where the Kürschner or Hafenhaus stood up to 1955. The striking building opposite is the Klösterle, originally the monastery church for a bare-footed order of monks. After the Reformation the town used it to store grain, and today it is partly used for storage but much more importantly as the municipal hall for major events. The beautiful main entrance door dates from the time when the building was converted in 1586. The white building opposite is the Kaisheimer Haus, which served from 1278 to 1803 as the main store for the Imperial monastery of Kaisheim, later becoming the county court and administrative headquarters, and is now once again the local courthouse. The next street, Tändelmarkt, leads us to the right into Nonnengasse and Manggasse, which we will now follow to the left. By crossing the Vorderer Gerbergasse („tanner's alley") we leave the oldest and most crowded part of the town. Romantic, steep-gabled Gerberhäuser (tanners' houses) on our left (No. 23) and right (No. 2) bear witness to the comfortable standard of living of the Nördlingen craftsmen of those days. At the western end of this street, and set off slightly to the right, is a barn-like building called the Holzhof, used today as the Rieskrater Museum. This collection is concerned with the meteor which collided with the Earth 15 million years ago and made the crater which is now the stretch of countryside called the Nördlingen Ries. Since the Apollo 14 and 17 astronauts completed their training here in 1970 we know that a major meteor, travelling at about 100,000 k.p.h., hit the earth and generated the heat which produced new geological formations similar to the craters of the moon.

At the end of the rear part of Gerbergasse is the beginning of the Spitalhof area, which is also continued on the far side of the Baldinger Strasse. The municipal museum is housed in one of these buildings, and documents the history of Nördlingen. Particularly impressive items in the collection include casts of the skull nests from the Often caves (about 11,000 BC), the flute-player from Roman times, the late Gothic Herlin altar, and the scenic display of pewter figures depicting the famous Battle of Nördlingen (1634).

A cobblestone slope leads down from the Herrngasse, still near the Spital, to the River Eger; this is called the Pferdeschwemme or „horse-dip". The Herrngasse finals opens into the Weinmarkt, where a fountain commemorates a courageous innkeeper's wife, Maria Holl, who despite having been subjected to agonising torture 56 times refused to give in and thus survived her trial as a witch. This bigotry had already cost 35 innocent people their lives, but thanks to Maria Holl a stop was put to this madness at least in Nördlingen.

The massive Hallgebäude (1543) once served as a warehouse for salt, wine, and grain. From the Neubaugasse we turn off next to the imposing half-timbered

Rieskrater-Museum: Depiction of the meteorite impact 15 million years ago.

St George's church: the nave

Winter'schen Haus into the Bräugasse and continue, keeping well to the left, until we reach the Herrgottskirche or St Salvator's church. This was consecrated in 1442 as the Carmelite's monastery church, but rather fundamentally altered in 1829. Nevertheless, the figures of the prophets in the opening of the west door are still well worth seeing, as are the wall frescoes, the High Altar, the bas-reliefs around the pulpit, and the „Miracle of the Host" painting. All these works of art date from the 15th century.
The Basteigasse leads us to the town walls with the Alte Bastei, which nowadays serves as an open-air theatre. We follow the defences to the Reimlinger Tor, which has been preserved complete with its outer bulwarks. Passing by the Ellinger Haus, once a storage house for the Deutscher Orden, we cross the Reimlinger Strasse and the Schöfflesmarkt to take the shortest route to St George's church. Its 90-metre tall tower, the „Daniel", will guide us. Dedicated in 1505 as one of the largest churches of its kind in southern Germany, it contains a ba-

The High Altar

Magnificent half-timbering on the Winter'schen House.

Old town lane in Nördlingen with "Daniel".

roque-style High Altar with late Gothic sculpture and altar panels and a late Gothic font. Anyone who would like a really good view out over the old town centre should choose a fine day and clamber the 350 stairs to the walkway round the top of the tower. From here, the watchman in the tower calls out his traditional medieval cry every half-hour, from 10.00 pm to midnight: „So, G'sell, so!" (very roughly: „All's well, fellows, all's well!"). Climbing and descending from the tower we encounter the old treadmill with which the watchmen and „fire warning" men pulled a basket up on a rope containing their nightly rations. From Nördlingen, before travelling further south-eastwards along the B 25 to Harburg (17 kilometres), it is well worth travelling the extra 15 kilometres to visit Holheim, the next village south-westwards (Stone Age caverns), and then swing southwards through Christgarten (Bavaria's smallest parish, Gothic Carthusian choir) and Mönchsdeggingen (Benedictine abbey, baroque church with horizontal organ dating from 1693), before returning to the B 25. There is a second possible excursion, a visit to the little town of Wemding, 17 kilometres east of Nördlingen, where it is worth looking at the market square, the town defences, the parish church, and the nearby pilgrimage church of Maria Brünnlein in the rococo style. From Wemding a road runs directly southwards to Harburg.

Harburg

The small medieval town of Harburg is squeezed onto the steep slope between the River Wörnitz and the Burgberg, the hill on which the massive fortress stands. When it was first mentioned in records in 1150 it was still in the possession of the Staufer emperors, having been built to secure the trading route from Augsburg to Nuremberg. 100 years later it was pledged to, and then taken over by, the Counts of Oettingen, together with the town, and it is still today in the hands of the same family. Never once conquered during the whole of its long history, it is now one of the best preserved castles in Germany.

Above the small town of the same name the mighty Harburg sits enthroned upon the Burgberg. Since 1250 it has been in possession of the Counts of Oettingen.

Because of the cramped space, the Romantic Road in the vicinity of the castle has to be led through a tunnel 300 metres long. Just before the tunnel, a road climbs up to the right to a car-park below the castle, entrance to which is covered by high walls with a walkway and arrow-slits, and a double gate-tower. The wooden portcullis with

Tourist information: Tourist Office,
Schloßstrasse 1, 86655 Harburg, tel. 09080/9699-0, fax 9699-30.
Opening hours: Castle, *16th March to 31st October, from 9:00 am - 17:00 pm without Monday (October 9:30 - 16:30 pm)*
Sightseeing visits after season (Nov. till middle of March)
Harburg Castle: *arrangements tel. 09080/9686-0.*
Fürst Wallerstein, *Schlösser & Museen, Burgstraße 1, 86655 Harburg,*
Internet: http://www. fuerst wallerstein.de, e-mail: schloesser@fuerst wallerstein.de

View of the upper castle courtyard with battlements, Water Tower, Baker's Building, Princely House, Banquet Hall, and well as seen from the Granary (left to right).

its iron tips is still preserved in the inner gate-tower. Around the inner castle courtyard are the Burgschenke or tavern, the Saalbau with a banqueting hall, the Fürstenbau in which the princes lived, the castle chapel, and the Hungerturm (13th century) which served as the castle keep and is at the same time the oldest part of the castle. A tour through the buildings leads to the priceless tombs of the Counts of Oettingen, and lasts a good half-hour.
From the castle hill the visitor has a fine view across the old town centre of Harburg and the meandering course of the Wörnitz, the river that marks the frontier between the Swabian and the Frankish Alb.

The car-driver can now travel down through narrow streets to the Wörnitz, where he can discover unique views particularly in the vicinity of the old stone-arched bridge (1712) with its seven arches, and the old houses huddling below the castle. However, he should explore the old town centre on foot and enjoy the lovely half-timbered houses, such as the former rectory and the town hall. Harburg's coat-of-arms consist of a black eagle with red weapons, indicating the town's origins as the Emperor's property.

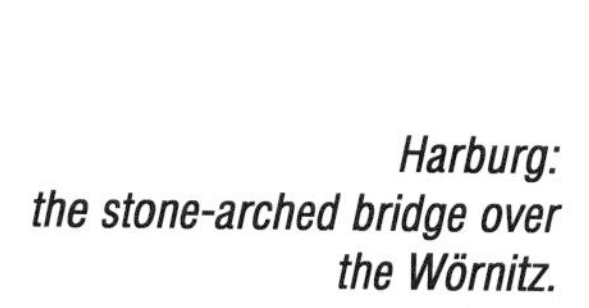

*Harburg:
the stone-arched bridge over
the Wörnitz.*

In the Land of the Counts and Princes of Oettingen-Wallerstein

Where History and Hospitally Meet

Wallerstein Castle An exquisite collection of porcelain and glassware, Royal Stables Museum in the Princely Riding School.
Phone: +49 9081/782285

Brewery Pub "Fürstlicher Keller" in Wallerstein with seating for more than 100 persons in the *Landsknechtsaal.*
Phone: +49 9081/79860

Baldern Castle an extensive collection of weaponry and exhibition rooms worth seeing. Phone: +49 7362/9688-0

Castle Pub at the Royal Stables, at Baldern Castle, seating for 120, company parties, special events, hot meals served all day!
Phone: +49 7362/9688-0

Harburg Castle one of Southern Germany's oldest, best-preserved, and largest castles.
Phone: +49 9080/96860

Harburg Castle Restaurant
with terrace and a cozy atmosphere.
Phone: +49 9080/1504

Eisbrunn Forest Restauran
near Harburg Castle.
Hall with seating for 120, sea
ing for 500 outdoors.
Phone: +49 9003/1555

Donauwörth

Donauwörth, a town of 20,000 inhabitants, stands at the confluence of the Wörnitz and the Danube. It originated as a fishing village on an island in the Wörnitz called Wörth, and when the first bridge was built across the Danube to carry the Augsburg-Nuremberg trading route the village of „Werd", later „Schwäbischwörth", gained in importance and was granted charter rights in 1193. From 1301 to 1607 it was a Free Imperial City and a significant trading centre, before being annexed by Bavaria.
The backbone of the historical old town centre is the Reichsstrasse, running from the town hall to the Fuggerhaus. It is an imposing street, the buildings along it forming a complete entity, and one of the most beautiful in the whole of southern Germany. Because of its great width it used to be called Oberer Markt and Unterer Markt, and was formed part of the main market street in the Middle Ages. The town hall has stood without interruption since 1236, although it has often been enlarged and altered. Above the main entrance doorway with its harmonious double stairway is the coat-of-arms as granted to the town by Karl V. in 1530. A Glockenspiel or carillon sounds out at 11.00 am and 4.00 pm every day with the melody „Die Sonne muss scheinen" („The sun must shine") from the opera „The Magic Fiddle" by Werner Egk (1901 - 1983). A fountain in the Rathausstrasse is also dedicated to this Donauwörth composer.
Along the Kapellgasse stand the Bürgerspital with its church (17th century) and the former house of the Deutscher Orden order of chivalry, a classical-style building containing a late-baroque banqueting hall. Glancing back towards the Rathausplatz we see a tall, half-timbered building, the upper floors of which project a long way forward. It stands in the Spitalgasse, at the far end of which the Riedertor leads us out across a bridge to the island called „Ried", which was the original settlement. Both this gateway and the Hintermeierhaus (formerly Fischerhaus, 15th century) on the island of Wörth contain historic collections. A footpath leads along the defensive wall from the Riedtor to the romantic Färbertörl, where one could almost forget the grim military purpose for which it was originally built.
Along the Reichsstrasse we pass by the Tanzhaus (15th century), dating from the days when this was an Imperial city, the ground floor of which was used at the front as bakers' and fish shops and

Tourist information: Municipal Tourist Office,
Rathausgasse 1, 86609 Donauwörth, tel. 0906/789151,
Internet: http://www.donauwoerth.de, e-mail: stadt@donauwoerth.de
Käthe Kruse dolls' museum: *April to October, every day except Mondays, from 2.00 to 5.00 pm; November to March, on Wednesdays, Saturdays, Sundays, and public holidays from 2.00 to 5.00 pm.*
Werner Egk Meeting House: *all year round, on Wednesdays, Saturdays, Sundays, and public holidays from 2.00 to 5.00 pm.*
Haus der Stadtgeschichte: *all year round, on Saturdays, Sundays, and public holidays from 2.00 to 5.00 pm.* ***Archaeological museum:*** *all year round, on Saturdays, Sundays, and public holidays from 2.00 to 5.00 pm.*
Museum of local arts and crafts on Ried island: *May to September, on Saturdays, Sundays, and public holidays from 2.00 to 5.00 pm.*
Lovriner Heimatstube: *as for museum of local arts and crafts.*

◀ *Former monastery of the Holy Cross.*

The romantic Färbertörl.

▼ *Infirmary barracks on the old town wall.*

at the rear as a market hall. The town used the upper floor on market days for merchants' stands, and on high days and holidays as a dance floor.
Diagonally opposite is the late-Gothic brick Minster (1444-1461). The biggest church bell in the whole of Swabia has hung in its belfry since 1512; it weighs 6½ tons and is called „Pummerin". It is worth climbing to the top of the church tower just for the magnificent view, and inside the church the soaring sacrament house and the late-Gothic frescoes are also worth a visit.
On our way to the two-storey Fuggerhaus we encounter a modern fountain (1977, Prof. Hans Wimmer) crowned by an eagle and with a column commemorating the main phases in the history of the town. The Renaissance building at the end of the Reichsstrasse is nowadays the Landratsamt or County Council headquarters, but it was built t in 1537-39 by Anton Fugger and was used in 1632, during the Thirty Years War, as headquarters by Gustav Adolf of Sweden and his consort, and later by the „Winter King" and by the Emperor Karl VI (1711).
We reach a particularly picturesque remnant of the medieval defensive wall with the round water-tower and the Invalidenkaserne or „infirmary barracks" (18th century) via the Pflegestrasse, then taking the first side-street to the left. The Heilig-Kreuz-Strasse, on the other hand, leads us to the district which used to be an extensive monastery complex surrounding the late-baroque Heilig-Kreuz-Kirche, the church of the Holy Cross. This harmonious structure was built in 1717-22 under the supervision of the famous architect from Wessobrunn, Joseph Schmuzer. Roman-style decorations can still be seen on the lower part of the tower, dating from the time when the first church was built on this site (1128). 73 metres above it stands the rococo cupola of the present-day building, with its many soaring curves.
The church doorway is artistically decorated with carvings, as are the eight altars, the choir stalls, and the pew ends. The tasteful and discreet stucco decorations framing the ceiling frescoes are

The massive Riedertor used to form part of the town's defences, and nowadays houses a museum illustrating the history of the town.

likewise the products of Wessobrunn master-craftsmen, and so is the High Altar, which came from the brother of the architect of the church. On the western side of the nave, a beautiful wrought-iron grille protects the gravestone of Maria, Duchess of Brabant. This unfortunately lady was beheaded in 1256 on the orders of her husband, Duke Ludwig the Harsh, because she was falsely suspected of infidelity. A flight of steps leads down to the crypt chapel, the ceiling of which is luxuriantly decorated with stucco. An artistic wrought-iron grill protects the two altars (1705) in the background; the left-hand one contains the Roman-style Kreuzpartikeltafel (11th century) contained in an elaborate baroque frame (1716). The parts of Christ's cross which are preserved here are to this day the reason for pilgrimages to this church, as also were the Pieta (early 16th century) on the right-hand altar. A further sight worth noting is the tombstone of Abbot Amandus Roels, who had the monastery and the church rebuilt. Further old tombstones and also sizeable baroque statues stand in the crossing, to which a door in the crypt chapel leads.

From Donauwörth to Augsburg is 50 kilometres, and the modern B 2 road is at the same time the Romantic Road. A possible diversion, involving and additional 27 kilometres or so, follows the B 16 south-westwards to Höchstadt (castle, museum of local arts and crafts, Prince Eugen monument) and Dillingen (Basilica of St Peter, seminary church of St Maria of the Ascension, magnificent Goldener Saal hall and Hiaslturm, the last resting place of the notorious huntsman and brigand Hiasl). The road south-eastwards through Wertingen and Biberach (baroque pilgrimage church with Roman-style crucifix, known to Swabians as the „Lieb's Herrgöttle" or „Our Dear Lord" of Biberach) takes us back onto the Romantic Road (B2) at Langwied.

The confluence of the Wörnitz and the Danube at Donauwörth.

Augsburg

The town has developed over a period of 2000 years, starting as a Roman military camp under the Emperor Augustus (15 BC), whose name lives on in that of the city. Because of its advantageous position at the cross-roads of major trading routes, it achieved considerable importance in the Middle Ages and world fame during the time of the wealthy Fugger family (around 1500) and the sea-faring dynasty of Weiser. Visits by the Emperor and sessions of the Reichstag or Imperial Parliament became everyday events, famous artists worked in the city, and it advanced during the Renaissance to become a centre of architecture, music, and painting. Today it is the third largest city in Bavaria and also a university city and the centre of the government district of Swabia, quite apart from also being a major commercial centre. The city's coat-of-arms contain a green pine-cone, a

Augsburg: The Hercules Fountain in front of the former Benedictine abbey church of St Ulrich and St Afra, easily recognised by its 93-metre tall „onion" tower.

Tourist information:
Bahnhofstrasse 7 and Rathausplatz, 86150 Augsburg,
PO Box 102560, 86015 Augsburg, tel. 0821 / 50207-0, fax 50207-45,
Internet: http://www.regio.augsburg.de, e-mail: stadtfuehrungen@regio.augsburg.de
Opening times of museums:
Closed on Mondays and Tuesdays.
Open Wednesday to Sunday from 10:00 am to 4:00 pm.

reminder of the past when Augsburg was a Roman provincial capital, just as the names of the Augsburg Confession and the Augsburg Religious Peace remind us of its significance during the time of the Reformation.

If a visitor were to try to explore all the sights worth seeing in this city, he would need several weeks. To start with, he has a choice of 15 museums and art galleries. However, just like the bus-tour of the city that runs every day and takes just over 2½ hours, we will have to limit ourselves to the main historical buildings. The route has been signposted by the city's Tourist Information Office with arrows on a green background, and can therefore be started at any convenient point, but it should be noted that a downwards-pointing arrow is meant to be pointing in the opposite direction to the way the onlooker is facing - that is, he has to turn round and go back. Anyone who has too little time to spare for the complete tour ought at least look at the highlights: the Rathaus or town hall with its Goldener Saal, the Fugger palace, the cathedral, and St Anna's church.

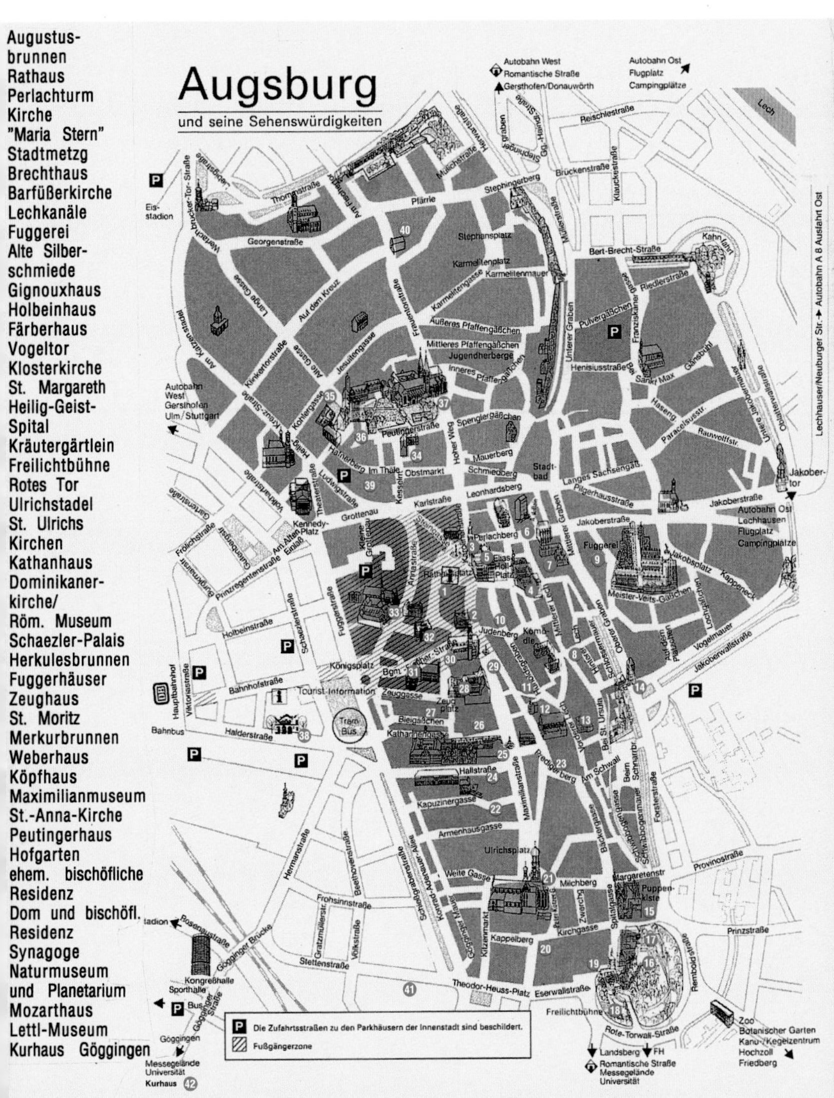

On the occasion of the city's 1600th jubilee in 1594, the city had the Augustus fountain ❶ erected in front of the town hall to the honour of its founder. The four figures around the basin symbolise the four rivers which have from the earliest days provided the vital water power for Augsburg craft enterprises. The Rathaus ❷ was built by the most famous of all local architects, Elias Holl, between 1615 and 1620. It is one of the most beautiful and significant buildings of the Renaissance, other than churches, anywhere north of the Alps. The Goldener Saal is unique with its sumptuous interior: magnificent doorways, wall-paintings, and an artistic cassetted ceiling. Augsburg's second landmark after the Rathaus is the nearby Perlachturm ❸; towering over the medieval core of the former defensive tower, and likewise designed by Elias Holl, the upper storeys carry the lantern belfry and are topped by the Welsche Haube, a typical feature of Augsburg. From the walkway around the top of the 70-metre tall tower there is a magnificent view over the old centre of the town. The arrows on the green signposts now lead us to a church, Maria Stern ❹, once the chapel of the Franciscan monastery. Built in 1574 - 76 under the direction of Johannes Holl, the father of the builder of the Rathaus, this was the first tower to be capped with a Welsche Haube, which is also known as an „Augsburg onion". It is to the younger Holl that Augsburg owes the former guild and market hall of the butchers, the Stadtmetzg ❺, with its harmonious main façade. The building was cooled by two underground channels diverted from the River Lech, which also served the purpose of waste disposal - in those days a very progressive development.

The city had the Brechthaus ❻ arranged in 1984 as a memorial for the writer, who was born here. A little further on, a red sign suggests a diversion from the main circuit to the Barfüsserkirche ❼, a Gothic church (1407-1411) which contains a priceless interior and a memorable crossing with a lace fan vaulting.

The part of the city we are now standing in is the Lechviertel, formerly a foregate, which takes its name from the branch of the River Lech ❽ which even in Roman times was diverted here. The flow of the water principally served as a source of power for mills and craft enterprises. No less than 15 of them can be explored here as part of the special „Craftsmen's Street", but it is advisable to enquire first at the Tourist Information Office about the opening hours. A further place to explore is the Handwerkermuseum or craftsmen's museum, near Point 17 on the city-history circuit, where some 40 different skilled trades are on show together with their historical development.

One of the most striking buildings in the city is the Fuggerei ❾, the oldest alms houses anywhere in the world, so called because they were built by the wealthy Fugger family. They were endowed in 1516 by Jakob Fugger the Wealthy and his brothers, and consist of 67 cottages containing 147 small apartments, a church, a fountain, and a surrounding wall with gateways, in effect a town within a town. According to the stipulations made at the time, the inhabitants must even today be poor, of blameless behaviour, citizens of Augsburg, and Catholic. They pay an annual rent of DM 1.72, the equivalent of one Rhinish Guilder, and have to say a prayer three times a day for the founder.

The way back to the centre leads, as the red signs show, to the old silver-smithy ❿ in the Pfladergasse, and then along the main circuit past the Gignouxhaus ⓫ (1765, a beautiful manufacturer's house in rococo style, nowadays „Komödie", the Holbeinhaus ⓬ in which Hans Holbein Senior lived, and the city's last Färberhaus ⓭ or dyer's house, to the Vogeltor ⓮, a Gothic city

▲ *The „Fuggerei“, the world's oldest alms houses, built from 1516 onwards by Jakob Fugger „the Wealthy“ and his brothers.*

„Fuggerei“: the eternal battle between Good and Evil. ▶

gate (1445). On our way to the southernmost tip of the city we go pass the Schwallech, with its authentic recreation of a wooden water-wheel. In the Margarethenstrasse stands the former abbey church of St Margareth ⓯ (1521, rebuilt in 1720), alongside which is the abbey courtyard with its open tree-line walkway. Further southwards again, another red sign suggests a diversion to the Heilig.Geist-Spital ⓰ or Hospice of the Holy Ghost, a late work by Elias Holl with an imposing internal courtyard.
The most southerly, and also the strong-

Famous Augsburg personalities: figures in the „Puppenkiste".

est, of the defensive bulwarks was the Rote-Tor-Bastei, where nowadays a herb garden ⑰ and an open-air theatre ⑱ take the place of the former moat - now, happily, no longer required. The Rotes Tor ⑲ dates from 1622, redesigned by Elias Holl, nowadays forms part of a romantic park.

Yet another red signposts suggests that we turn off to the left from the Kirchgasse, the end of which we will reach after we have visited the Ulrichstadel ⑳. This was the stables and hay-barn of the Benedictine abbey of St Ulrich and St Afra ㉑, which in its day was subordinate only to the Emperor. The late-Gothic basilica possesses a valuable interior, in both the Renaissance and the baroque style, and a former sermon hall which today is the Evangelical church of St Ulrich. Whilst the Maximilianstrasse leads us further northwards, we now pass the Kapuzinergasse (No. 10 is a house, Kathanhaus) ㉒, with a beautifully painted exterior, and the short road leading to the Dominican church ㉓ containing the Roman museum. On the left-hand side of the street stands one of Augsburg's most impressive rococo palaces, the Schaezler-Palais ㉔. Apart from its magnificent banqueting hall, 23 metres long and rich in carvings and stucco decorations, wall mirrors and ceiling frescoes, it is nowadays also the home of the German Baroque Gallery and the State Gallery.

The nearby Herkulesbrunnen ㉕ was created in about 1600, as was the next foun-

Rotes Tor and the tower of the church of St Ulrich.

Schaezler-Palais: the imposing town mansion of a banker, today the home of the German Baroque Gallery and the State Gallery.

tain, the Merkurbrunnen ㉙. Both are the work of the Dutch artist Adrian de Vries, but between the two we should look at the Fuggerhäuser ㉖, built in 1512-15 as residential homes and business premises by Jakob Fugger, with their charming internal courtyards, and at the Zeughaus ㉗ built as a warehouse in 1607 (E. Holl, magnificent façade) and the former monastic foundation, the Chorherrenstift St Moritz ㉘, with the remains of its baroque interior. Passing by the reconstructed, brightly coloured Zunfthaus der Weber ㉚ or weavers' guild hall of 1389, we come to the Köpfhaus ㉛, created like the Fuggerhäuser in the 16th century by incorporating and converting a number of smaller houses. Immediately adjacent are a monument (to Hans Jakob Fugger) and the Welserhaus to remind us of the two families which once were the most powerful ones in Augsburg. The Bürgerhaus, which originally had a painted exterior, and is now the

Augsburg Cathedral boasts a priceless interior, medieval coloured glass, frescoes, and panel paintings.

Maximilian-Museum, was built in 1546 and now houses a collection of artistic exhibits illustrating the history of the city. We reach another highlight in a circuit which is brim full of sights worth seeing when we get to St Anna's church ㉝. This former Carmelite monastery church (1321, enlarged in the 15th century) contains Gothic wall decorations and valuable paintings, including some by Lucas Cranach the Elder, and the sepulchre chapel of the Fuggers which they used from 1509 to 1518. In the latter year, Martin Luther stayed in the adjoining monastery for the period of his negotiations with the Papal Legate Cajetan. As the church was used for Evangelical services from 1525 onwards, the Fuggers gave up their sepulchre chapel. Whilst the Peutingerhaus ㉞ (16th century, fine rococo façade dating from 1763) and the garden of the bishops' palace ㉟ lie a little off to one side of our main route, we will concentrate on the Residenz am Fronhof ㊱, near the cathedral. The tower is all that has been preserved from the medieval Fronhof; the remaining buildings date from the 18th century, and are now used as a residence by the government of Swabia. On 25th June 1530 the „Augsburg Confession" was promulgated in the Chapter Room, which was then still in existence; this is the basic confession of the Lutheran church. Only a few metres separate the bishops' palace from their own church, the cathedral ㊲, which was first mentioned in historical records as long ago as 823. The crypt (10th century) is nearly as old as the records, and the coloured glass paintings (12th century) are amongst the oldest in Germany. Ceiling and wall frescoes from the Roman and Gothic periods, panel paintings by Hans Holbein Senior, and a bronze door (about 1356, with 35 bas-relief illustrations) make the cathedral a treat for the eyes of any lover of church art.

A view from the north towards the Perlachturm, the Perlach town hall, and St Ulrich's church.

Friedberg

The B 300 main road intersects with the actual Romantic Road outside St Ulrich's church in Augsburg, and this takes us 7 kilometres eastwards to the former fortified town of Friedberg. It was created in 1264 as the frontier fortifications of the Dukes of Wittelsbach mainly against the three Augsburg territories of the Free Imperial City, the See, and the Imperial Benedictine monastery of St Ulrich and

Friedberg: Marienplatz with town hall and fountain.

Tourist information: Friedberg Municipal Tourist Office,
Marienplatz 14, 86316 Friedberg, tel. 0821/6002-213, fax 6002-205.
Opening times of museum:
Wednesday 2:00 pm - 4:00 pm on Sundays and publisc holidays 10:00 am 12:00 pm also by prior arrangements.

St Afra, but also against the Swabians generally. The sturdy defensive walls, bastions, and towers look down on us and welcome us from a long way away. The defences are still partly preserved today; they were built at the beginning of the 15th century, as a late-Gothic plaque in the west wall of St Jacob's church (19th century) commemorates. Apart from the remains of the town wall, principally the part in the south-west corner, the most pleasing feature is the central Marienplatz with its pretty fountain, the Mariensäule column, and the neat town hall, built by the citizens of Friedberg in 1974 in the style of Augsburg's Elias Holl. The palace up above Friedberg was built in 1552 - 59 on the site of a 13th century Wittelsbach castle, and today houses a museum of local arts and crafts. Among other things, it offers a remarkable collection illustrating the faience manufacture which was still in operation here in until recent times, with the once-famous Friedberg clocks and a wide selection of Friedberg handiwork.

East of the centre of the town lies the pilgrimage church of Hergottsruh, which takes its name („The Peace of God") from the famous Picture of Grace (about 1496), which shows an Jesus resting, exhausted from carrying the Cross. This church was built in 1731-35, and its particularly pleasing feature is its vaulted ceiling, which seems to float weightlessly with its outstanding cupola frescoes and artistic stucco work from the Wessobrunn master Feichtmayr. Amongst the altars, those particularly worth mentioning are the Bruderschaftsaltar, or altar of fraternity, and the Gnadenaltar, or Altar of Grace, which has the picture described above. This was for centuries the reason for which innumerable pilgrims came to this church. A sight worth seeing outside the town is the chapel of „St Afra in the Fields", where a church has stood since 978. The present one dates from the first few years of the 18th century, and contains memorable stucco work from the renowned artist Schmuzer.

The pilgrimage church of Herrgottsruh: the Picture of Grace.

Returning to Augsburg, we reach the B 17 again and turn southwards, thus avoiding the modern by-pass, and pass through various interesting towns and villages: Haunstetten (St Mary's chapel), Klosterlechfeld, where a chapel of pilgrimage (1603, Elias Holl) commemorates the legendary battle here in 955 when the Emperor Otto the Great defeated the Hungarians and drove them out of Central Europe once and for all.

After a total of 45 kilometres we arrive in Landsberg. Because the old town centre is cramped and crowded, it is advisable to park in the underground garage, from where we need barely 5 minutes to reach the centre.

Landsberg

The Schlossberg, a steep hill above the crossing-point of the River Lech, has often been the site of a settlement on account of its favourable position. Excavations indicate a bronze-age settlement (about 1800 - 1200 BC) and a pottery-age settlement (about 1250 - 750 BC), as well as one in the later Roman era (300-400 AD). Henry the Lion then had a castle, the „Landespurch", built to secure the Salt Road, which led from Reichenhall to Lake Constance. The „salt tax" which had to be paid contributed substantially to the wealth of the town in

Landsberg: the Hauptplatz with the market fountain, dominated by a statue of the Virgin Mary. Behind it is the rich façade of the baroque town hall.

Tourist information: Landsberg Municipal Culture and Tourist Office, *Hauptplatz 1, 86896 Landsberg am Lech, tel. 08191/128-246, fax 128-160, Internet: http://www.landsberg.de, e-mail: stadt_LL@landsberg.de*
Bayertor: *Open May to October, every day, 10 am to 12 noon and 2 to 5 pm.*
Altes Rathaus: *May to October, Mon. to Fri., 8 am to 6 pm; Sat., Sun., and public holidays 10 am to 12 noon and 2 to 5 pm; Nov. to April, Mon. to Thursdays, 8 am to 12 noon and 2 to 5 pm, Fridays 8 am to 12.30 pm.*
Mutterturm, *every day, 2.00 to 5.00 pm, closed on Mondays and public holidays.*
Herkomer museum, *every day, 2.00 to 5.00 pm, closed on Mondays and public holidays.*

the Middle Ages. Even today, Landsberg has a very central location and can be very easily reached by all means of transport, in particular because of the north-south route of the B 17 and the E 54 (or A 96) motorway now being built from Munich to Lindau.

The Municipal Tourist Office has drawn up a town sight-seeing circuit which takes about 1½ hours on foot and sign-posted it with the stylised symbol „LL" (for „Landsberg am Lech", the same abbreviation as on the car number-plates) and six circular discs. Optional extensions to the circuit are marked with rings instead of discs. It should be noted that the complete circuit involves climbing considerable heights and descending again, and so requires more physical effort than most such circuits in other towns.

Let us start here, as usual, in the centre, on the broad Hauptplatz, in the middle of which the old town hall once stood. The present-day Rathaus (about 1700) is integrated into the western row of houses, but stands out because of its richly decorated stucco façade. It is a piece of work from the same architect as the one who created the famous Wieskirche (50 kilometres to the south, and see Chapter 24)

1. Rathaus; 2. Klosterkirche; 3. Lechwehr; 5. Färbertor; 6. Bäckertor; 7. St John's church; 8. Historical shoe museum; 9. Sandauer Tor; 10. Dachlturm; 11. Pulverturm (magazine); 12. City parish church; 13. Arkadenhof; 14. New municipal museum; 15. Heilig-Kreuz-Kirche; 16. Bayertor; 17. Jungfernsprung; 18. Nonnenturm; 19. Schmalzturm; 20. Mutterturm; 21. Herkomermuseum

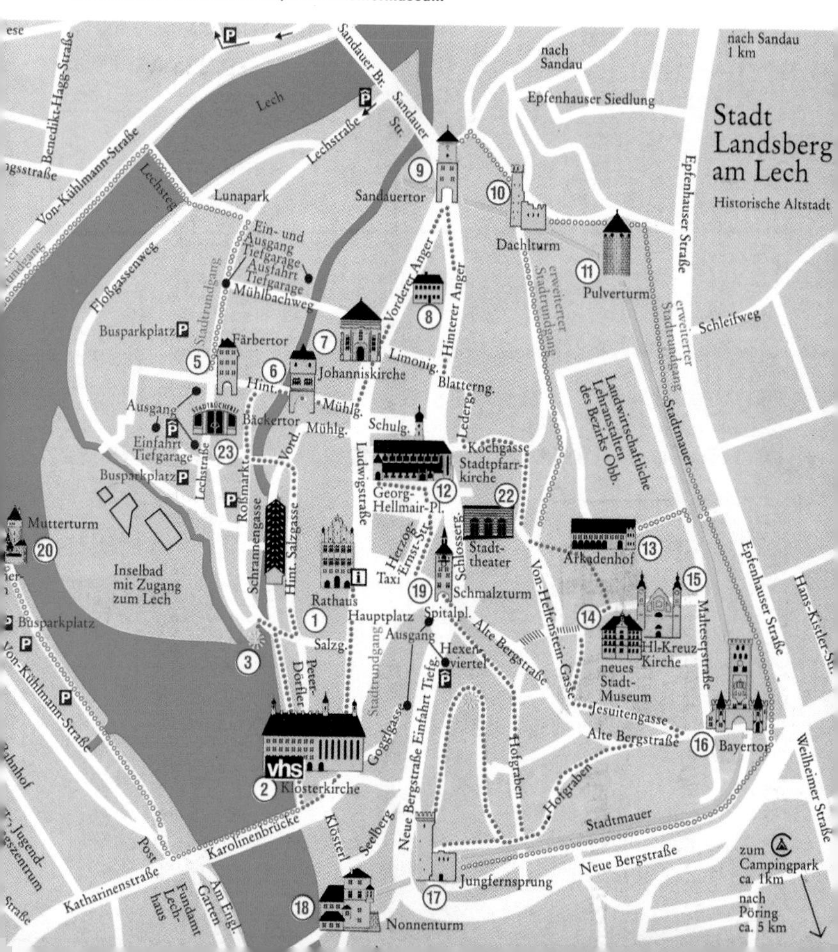

Landsberg: A view across the Wehr to the east bank of the River Lech. The „onion tower" belongs to the municipal parish church.

- Dominikus Zimmermann, who also did the stucco work in the upper storey. It was under his direction that St John's church in Landsberg was built in 1752, and he was mayor from 1749 to 1754, almost exactly the period of time when he was supervising the building of his life's work, the famous Wieskirche (1746-54). A beautiful fountain (1783) stands in front of the town hall with a statue of the Virgin Mary.

The Hubert von Herkomer Strasse leads us past the former Klosterkirche or monastery church (built from 1740 onwards to plans from Johann Baptiste Gunetzerhainer) and on down to the River Lech. Here it is worth making a short diversion across the bridge and along the promenade to the right, to gain a fine view of the city. One curious tower building stands on the west bank - the Mutterturm, built at the end of the 19th century as the residence and studio of the painter and draftsman Hubert von Herkomer. A collection of his work can still be seen exhibited here. Returning to the bridge, we keep over to the left and, near the Inselbad, turn off into the Hintere Salzgasse. On our left, the uniform row of houses make the narrowness of the plots very clear on which the buildings stand between the river and the steep slope. At the end of the row, we keep on the left-hand side and then, on the right-hand side, pass two former gateway towers along the Rossmarkt. Whilst the outer Fäbertor was built in about 1560, when the town was being expanded, the Bäckertor has been standing here behind the canalised section of

the River Lech since the 15th century. It leads us up to the Vorderer Anger, which we follow to the left. The church of St John, mentioned before, fits perfectly into the overall view of the town, which has grown harmoniously over the centuries, and with the Sandauer Tor (about 1630). Immediately adjacent to this north gate of the town is the Staffingerhof, once the home of the Landsberger Bund, an organisation founded in 1556 and which existed until 1599 with the aim of defending the town from Protestantism. After this the building, together with its lovely Arkadenhof, passed into the possession of the Dukes of Bavaria and was used as a riding school. Going along the Hinterer Anger, we come to the massive parish church of St Mary of the Ascension (15th century). It possesses some magnificent glass windows (16th century) and stucco work, as well as carvings by Lorenz Luidl (the Palm Sunday donkey and the Madonna of Hans Multscher).
Steps now help us to clamber upwards to the site of the former Jesuit monastery. Next to the doorway of the Heilig-Kreuz-Kirche (1752-54) is the entrance to the beautiful Arkadenhof, which belonged to the Jesuit college. The church, plain and undecorated on the outside, overwhelms the visitor with the magnificence of the baroque and rococo interior, with ornamental stucco and frescoes, paintings, and the fine wood carvings of the confessional boxes. The city has arranged its museum in the former Jesuit school. In additional to numerous testimony to the life of the citizens, it also possesses works of art collected together from numerous churches; Landsberg possessed 11 of them during the rococo age, when its population was only 2,000.

The 30-metre tall Mutterturm was built in 1884-88.

One of the most valuable pieces is a late Gothic sculpture depicting the coronation of the Virgin Mary.
The circuit now leads us on uphill to the rectangular lines of the Bayertor, a 36-metre tall tower provides an unrestricted view out over the old town and, if the weather permits, across to the serried ranks of the Alps. Outside the gate we follow the signs for the voluntary addition to the circuit and follow the neatly tended promenade outside the town wall to the Jungfernsprungturm (the „maiden's leap" tower). Returning a few yards to the Hofgraben we can re-enter the old town centre, where the houses are numbered according to a curious system which completely ignores their arrangement into streets. From our vantage point on the Schlossberg we can once

The imposing Bayertor (15th century) is one of the largest Gothic defensive towers belonging to town fortifications anywhere in Bavaria.

again enjoy the view before diving down through the picturesque, higgledy-piggledy Hexenviertel to the Schöner Turm or „beautiful tower". Because farmers passing through it sold such produce as goose-dripping, it is also known popularly as the Schmalzturm. This imposing defensive tower was built in the 13th century and was part of the oldest sections of the town defences. Our circuit ends when we reach the adjoining Hauptplatz.

It is perhaps not very surprising that a city so rich in history should maintain its old customs. In addition to the Belagerungsfest (a giant village fete celebrating the raising of a siege), the Christkindlmarkt (an open-air market and fairground during Advent), and processions in historical costume, the most celebrated is the Landsberger Ruethenfest which takes place every four years and draws large numbers of visitors from far and near. About 1,000 Landsberg children, many in historical costumes, act out town history together with grown-ups and bring the Middle Ages back to life.

The Sandauer Tor has guarded the ▶ northern entrance to the city for more than three hundred years.

▼ Landsberger „Ruethenfest", a children's event which takes place every four years (the next occasion will be in 2003).

Hohenfurch

Hohenfurch is only about 22 kilometres away to the south, along the B 17 main road. This also passes by the baroque tavern at Römerkessel, which invites the passer-by to stay an enjoy the view of the River Lech with its dams and lakes. It is also a good base for excursions to the Ammersee lake and to Diessen (monastery church with stucco work by Feuchtmayr and paintings by Tiepolo) and the monastery of Andechs (with a fine view, a rococo church, and a brewery and tavern operated by Benedictine monks).

The Romantic Road slices through the village of Hohenfurch, which invites the traveller to stay for a tranquil holiday amidst the beautiful surroundings of Upper Bavaria. Set amidst a huge number of magnificent churches and monasteries, it represents the northern gateway to the Pfaffenwinkel, a region in the foothills of the Alps particularly rich in church art. Hohenfurch has a particularly fine church in relation to its village status, with a tower and Choir dating from the 14th or 15th century. The Choir and the late-Gothic nave were rebuilt in about 1750 in the rococo style, and consecrated together with the three altars in 1754. The remainder of the interior likewise dates from about this time. The tall windows of the nave and the delicately shaded Wessobrunn stucco work make the interior bright and friendly, and shows off the frescoes, pictures, and carved figures particularly well.

A little way outside the village another church rises on a nearby hill - the late Roman-style chapel of St Ursula. It is not open to the public. We are now only 5 kilometres away from Schongau, the next spot on the Romantic Road.

The Madonna in Hohenfurch.

Information:
Ms Johanna Gerbl, Lechstrasse 4, 86978 Hohenfurch, tel. 08861/4423
Parish church:
the interior can only be viewed through a grille inside the door.
The key is available from the rectory.

Schongau

The town first originated where Altenstadt now stands, but the present settlement started in the 13th century on the hill which used to be rounded by the River Lech. It was granted municipal rights as long ago as 1331, and later received many other guaranteed privileges, which enabled it to develop into a significant centre of trade until the trading routes moved elsewhere as a result of the discovery of America and the sea routes to south-east Asia.

The romantic medieval hill town nowadays has about 12,000 inhabitants, the vast majority of whom live outside the town walls. As a place to park a car is a rarity within the town walls, we recommend car drivers to use the free car-park in the Amtsgerichtsgasse. From here it is not far along the Weinstrasse

Schongau: A view across the Marienplatz, named after the 8.50-metre tall fountain of St Mary, with the church of St Mary of the Ascension in the background.

Tourist information: Schongau Tourist Office, *Münzstrasse 5, PO Box 1322, 86953 Schongau, tel. 08861/7216 and 71444, fax 2626, Internet: http://www.schongau.de*

Opening times: Municipal museum: *Tue. to Sun., 10 am to 12 noon and 2 to 5 pm.*

Municipal parish church of St Mary of the Ascension, *every day from 8 am to 6 pm.*

to the present-day Rathaus ❶, built in 1922-26. We will now follow the circuit through the Gothic old town centre prepared by the Schongau tourist office. Opposite the town hall stands the municipal parish church of St Mary of the Ascension ❷, externally a rather plain building, with a tower and a Choir dating from the 17th century and a nave from 1751-53. The numerous frescoes and statues inside the church all relate to the life of the Blessed Virgin, and her statue also stands in the centre of the High Altar, amidst many others. The ceiling paintings in the Choir show the Holy Trinity welcoming the Virgin Mary into heaven, with the Holy Ghost shown as a knight-at-arms in rococo costume - although this form of depiction had been banned by Papal decree in 1745. South of the church is the broad Marienplatz, the southern boundary of which is formed by the stepped gable of the Ballenhaus ❹. This Gothic building (1419 and 1515) originally served as a warehouse, and until 1902 as the town hall,

The column of the fountain of St Mary in front of the stepped gable of the Ballenhaus, once a warehouse and later Schongau's town hall.

the richly decorated Ratsstube or council chamber being still preserved today. Its successor was the neighbouring Altes Rathaus ❸, which today houses the municipal music school, but had already been mentioned in historical records dating from 1580 as a tavern, the Gasthof zum Stern. It possesses charm-

ing stucco work by the Wessobrunn master Franz Schmuzer.
If we now turn back towards the Marienplatz, we can see on the right-hand side, near the fountain, the Tax Office ❺, which used to be the store and office for the monastery of Rottenbuch and later the Royal Bavarian Pensions Office. In the middle of the square is the 8.50-metre tall column of the Marienbrunnen ❻ with its rich decoration of coats-of-arms. It is a three dimensional history-lesson by the sculptor Bernd Schmitt, and dates from 1949. The Löwenstrasse comes in here from the west, and by going along this we come to the former Stadtapotheke ❼ or municipal pharmacy, which until about 1800 had been a brewery and tavern called the Drei Hasen. The romantic inner courtyard is particularly worth seeing.
If we turn off to the left at the end of the Löwenstrasse, and then take the next turning to the right, we will find ourselves facing the Frauentor ❽, which is mentioned in historical records as long ago as 1392. The wall paintings depicting the Mother of God were created by the mayor, Johann Pöllandt, in about 1700. On the other side of the gateway we now keep to the left along the defensive wall, which leads us to the Polizeidienerturm ❾, which is 17.25 metres tall and thus the tallest fortification in the town. In the old days it was the well-guarded gate that admitted last-minute guests or inhabitants returning home late. From here, the southernmost end of the old town centre, we have a fine view over the Lech and towards the Alps.
The next tower, the Eckturm ❿, is 15 metres tall, only slightly smaller than its neighbour. Returning to the old town centre through the broad Lechtorstrasse, we can turn off right and enter the Karmelitenstrasse, following it to its far end and passing the Steingadener Richterhaus ⓫ of 1492. Facing it, on the left-hand side, is the Holy Ghost Church ⓬, built in 1719 for the Carmelite monastery. They were actually an Order committed to poverty and begging, and their church as such is correspondingly modest, so that the seven fine altars, the priceless organ, and principally the magnificent pulpit, donated by a wealthy craftsman and his wife, dominate the interior completely.
Passing through the monastery building and patches of open ground, we catch frequent glimpses of the eastern part of the old defensive wall ⓭ where there are no defensive towers; the ground to the right was after all Bavaria. Our way lies straight ahead through the Amtsgerichtsstrasse until we have to follow a curve to the left past the

Town walls with walkway and tower gateway.

cemetery. This is where St Sebastian's church ⓮ stands, consecrated in 1774. In addition to three statues on the High Altar produced by mayor Pöllandt (1697), already mentioned, the stage-like Choir altar is also worth mentioning. The upper picture of the right-hand side-altar illustrates St Magnus fighting a dragon; he is the patron saints of gardens and fields, and protects them from pests. According to invoices from 17th and 18th century the pest officers, the Staff of this Saint was fetched several times from Füssen in attempt to master plagues of mice.

From the Obere Münzstrasse we turn right and look at the Münzgebäude ⓯, originally the „mint" or treasury and later used as a prison; today it is the police station. Schongau held the privilege of minting its own coins from 1331 to 1750, but the present building was not built until 1771.

Passing through the Königstor (1331) we can follow the way to the left, outside the town walls again, and soon see the Heiligkreuz pilgrimage church ⓰ at the bottom of the hills. Replacing an early wooden chapel, the main part of the present-day building was built by Joseph Schmuzer in 1690-93, as was an extension in 1725.

Our route now takes us to the Maxtor, which used to double as the castle gateway to the Schloss Schongau. A fresco above the gateway arch commemorates the granting of municipal rights by Emperor Ludwig the Bavarian in 1331. Above it stands Schloss Schongau ⓱, built in the 15th century as one of the Wittelsbachs' more minor residences, later becoming the residence of a county judge. A portrait hangs in front of the modern county council offices commemorating the fact that a well-known German politician called Franz-Josef Strauss once worked in this building. The Christophstrasse then brings us back to the Rathaus, but first we can spend a little time in the municipal museum ⓲. It is accommodated in a building which used to be the Erasmuskirche, and possesses a major collection of some 2,000 coins, which building workers found not very long ago in a pottery jar; they had been buried for safety during a siege in 1372.

Band in traditional Bavarian costume, high above the silhouette of Schongau.

Peiting

Markt Peiting is similar in size to its neighbour Schongau and only 4 kilometres away. The little town appears in historical records in 1055, when Count Welf IV had a new castle built on the Schlossberg; it then developed into the family residence of the southern German Welf dynasty and the central residence for the County of Peiting. When the Welf family finally died out, the town passed into the possession of the Staufers and later, in 1269, to the Wittelsbach dynasty. This made it part of Bavaria, although it retained its independence until 1343. Nowadays only the parish church of St Michael shows any traces of the town's grand past; the lower part of the tower and the columns beneath the altar date from the time when the first stone church was built, in about 1055. The font bears the date of 1331. The remaining parts of the building date from the 18th century, and are very plain and simple. However, the three rococo altars are worth looking at; they were acquired in 1803 from the monastery church of Rottenbuch when this was dissolved, and some have since had carved figures added to them; there are also fine confessional boxes and the pulpit. To accommodate the High Altar, which dominates the entire interior of the church even though in Rottenbuch it was only a side-altar, it was necessary to raise the whole vault of the Choir. This, as well as the flanking sculptures, was the work of Franz Xaver Schmädel, in 1758. The monumental crypt, formerly a mortuary, was built some time prior to 1350.
Only about 700 metres distant from the centre of this small town is the pilgrimage church of Maria Egg (about 1800), the appeal of which is its relatively rich interior.

In addition to the charms of rural life, the town offers many attractive leisure facilities and is a central base for walking tours through the dreamy marshland lakes and motor tours through the surrounding countryside. On clear days a trip to the Hohenpeissenberg (988 metres) is particularly warmly recommended, as there is a unique view from the top across the entire Herrgottswinkel with the Alps as a backcloth. There is also a pilgrimage chapel up here, with a Picture of Grace. From Peiting we can follow the B 23 main road southwards, towards the majestic mountains, to Rottenbuch (10 kilometres).

Peiting: the parish church of St Michael.

Tourist information: Markt Peiting Tourist Office, *Ammergauer Straße 2, 86971 Peiting, tel. 08861/6535, fax 59140, Internet: http://www.peiting.de*
Parish church of St Michael, *open only for services.*
Pilgrimage church of Maria Egg, *open every day from 7 am to 6.30 pm or when the bidding bell rings if earlier. Please use the side entrance by the graveyard.*

Rottenbuch

The tower of the former Augustine monastery, off-set from the nave of its church, greets the traveller from a long way off. This monastery is the successor to an earlier one, founded in 1073 by Duke Welf I but destroyed during the course of the Middle Ages. Around 1700, and later in about 1750, this magnificent new monastery building arose but work on it ceased abruptly in 1803 when the monasteries were dissolved and „secularised“. The former abbot, Herkulan Schweiger, succeeded with great effort and commitment in saving at least the monastery church with its tower, but the monastery itself survives only in the form of a few separate buildings such as the gateway and the brew-house.

Plain and simple on the outside, the church shows a convincing harmony of Roman, gothic, and baroque styles. Whilst the only remnants of the first stage of building of about 1100 are the foundations and the crossing, which are unusual for this region, the superstructure of nave and tower date from the

The remains preserved today of a monastery complex of Rottenbuch, with its central church, which once spread far more widely.

Tourist information: Rottenbuch Tourist Office,
Klosterhof 36 (in the town hall),
82401 Rottenbuch, tel. 08867/1464, fax 1858.
Office open on Mondays to Fridays, from 8.30 am to 12.00 noon.

The magnificent interior of the Gothic monastery church, with its magnificent frescoes and stucco work, altars, and sculptures of angels in the rococo style.

15th century. The church's present day appearance really only dates from 18th century, with in particular the luxuriant stucco work of J. Schmuzer and his son and the beautiful frescoes of Matthäus Günther. The lush magnificence of the Franz Xaver Schmädl interior (about 1750), which still inundates the interior despite the forced sale of the building in 1803, is augmented particularly by the numerous figures of angels, the organ case, the pulpit, the four side-altars, the figures of the founders, and the magnificent High Altar which he created. The crossing was simply walled off after 1803. In the right-hand part, now the

The Gothic tower of the monastery church with its classical cupola.

vestry, there used to be the side-altar which is now the High Altar in Peiting. One special jewel of Gothic church art can be seen in the first side-altar on the right, when seen from the Choir; a valuable late-Gothic Madonna (about 1483), handing fruit to the Christ-child.
Some 500 metres further east is where an octagonal chapel, the Frauenbrünnerl, was built in 1688; the name indicates its dedication to the Blessed Virgin and its position above a spring. On its altar there is a copy of a 15th century Gothic Madonna.
After a further 3 kilometres along the B 23, a narrow road branches off to the right in the direction of Füssen. However, we will first go a few metres further and turn right onto the car-park in front of the Echelsbach bridge, built in 1929 to cross the 76-metre deep and ancient gorge of the Ammer. The road over it, which here is part of the „German Alpine Road“ tourist route, leads to the well-known fresh-air and mud-bath spa town of Bayersoien and onward to Unterammergau (St Nicholas' church), Oberammergau (passion play theatre, church of St Peter and St Paul), Ettal (cloister with the church of St Mary of the Ascension) and finally to Garmisch Partenkirchen (36 kilometres).

The Echelsbach bridge crosses the ancient Ammer gorge.

Wildsteig

We, however, will branch off shortly before the bridge and continue another 3 kilometres along the Romantic Road to Wildsteig, a quiet community of hill farmers on the southern fringes of the Pfaffenwinkel region. Wildsteig is recognised as a healthy holiday area because of its position in the middle of a protected-landscape area with its rare plants and animals.

The attractive church, dedicated to St Jacob, was given its present shape in the second half of the 18th century. Outwardly as plain and modest as can be, the church's appealing feature is its light, friendly interior. The fine stucco work by the Wessobrunn master Thassilo Zöpf and his pupil Doll display features both of baroque and of classicism. The high-quality frescoes were painted by the Oberammergau artist Franz S. Zwinck, who earned himself the nickname of Luftmaler - an artist who paints with air. The High Altar is also worthy of note, with a picture by the painter Johann Degler (1666-1729), and the two outstanding late-Gothic accompanying figures which once decorated the Gothic High Altar in the monastery church in Rottenbuch.

2½ kilometres further on beyond Wildsteig, a narrow road off to the left leads to the „Wies".

Tourist information: Wildsteig Tourist Office,
Kirchbergstrasse 20a,
82409 Wildsteig, tel. 08867/409.

The "Wieskirche" Pilgrimage Church and Steingaden

The full name is Wallfahrtskirche zum Gegeisselten Heiland auf der Wies, or „Pilgrimage Church to Our Tortured Saviour on the Meadow", and suitably enough it appears as a plain, white church surrounded by meadows and in front of the dark backdrop of the mountains. What is such a magnificent church doing in the lonely midst of the forests and meadows and marshes? In 1730, two priests of the Prémont order, from the monastery of Steingaden, had prepared a „Tortured Saviour" from various wooden figures for the Good Friday procession. They covered the limbs of their figure with linen and painted it with red paint. Many people were upset by the statue, as it seemed to be too heavily „blood-stained", and in 1734 it disappeared into the loft of an inn-keeper in Steingaden. Only four years later, a relative of the inn-keeper took the figure away to her Wieshof, her „farm in the meadows", and held it in the greatest reverence, and it was in this same year that the „miracle of the meadows" happened; tears were seen on the face of the „Tortured Saviour". A surge of pilgrimage started, as pious pilgrims travelled even from Switzerland, Bohemia, the Tyrol, and Hungary to the field chapel, built in 1740. As the flood of pilgrims increased still further, the Abbot of Steingaden decided in 1745 to build a large pilgrimage church here. The Wessobrunn architect Dominikus Zimmermann, already 60 years old, succeeded in setting the crowning glory on his artistic creation by building the world-famous Wieskirche. He must have considered it in this way too, because although he lived another 12 years after it was completed he never again attempted a major church and lived in a small house close to his masterpiece until his death. However, this masterpiece made him immortal with its incomparable harmony of landscape and architecture on the outside and its architectural skill, its sculpture, and the paintings in the interior of this pilgrimage church. It floods over with light. His brother, Johann Baptist Zimmermann, court painter at the court of the Princes Elector in Munich, created the much admired ceiling frescoes with works that must surely be amongst the most beautiful of all rococo painting. Anton Sturm and Aegidius Verhelst worked as sculptors.

The High Altar, framed with columns, dominates the Choir and houses the famous Picture of Grace. The columns here look like marble but were in fact made of stucco, so that they could blend in with the architect's plan. The vaulted roof, 28 metres long and 18 wide, which looks like masonry, was in fact produced in wood to Dominikus Zimmermann's design. He thus saved weight, and could make taller and wider openings in the outside walls, and this explains the almost unearthly volume of light and the elegant, slender columns. The ceiling is completely flat, except for a cavetto of about 2.50 metres, but because of the perspective painting and sophisticated colouring looks like a genuine vault above the

Tourist information: Steingaden Tourist Office, *Schongauer Strasse 1, 86989 Steingaden, tel. 08862/200, fax 6470.*
Curatorium of the „Wieskirche" pilgrimage church:
86989 Steingaden-Wies, tel. 08862/501, fax 414.
The churches are open during daylight hours.

The baroque Wieskirche is the quintessence of a Bavarian rococo church, demonstrating perfect harmony between Nature and architecture.

oval shape of the nave. This curves out again towards the west, to create sufficient space for a gracefully curved organ loft, a treat for the eyes in white and gold.
Far more colourful features are the richly decorated, brilliant pulpit, probably also designed by Zimmermann, and opposite the Abbot's pew which forms and architectonic counterweight.
The secularisation of the monasteries in 1803 very nearly meant the irrevocable loss of the Wieskirche, which today is a UNESCO World Cultural Inheritance. After the dissolution of the monastery in Steingaden, it was to have been sold at auction, together with its entire interior, and demolished. Fortunately the highest bid only came to 800 guilders - it had cost 180,000 guilders to build - and the authorities in Munich decided this was not high enough. Members of the Steingaden monastery and the parish of Fronreiten were thus able to avert the worst.
We now travel another 5 kilometres, back to the main road and then in the direction of Füssen, to reach the resort of Steingaden. Before setting off on the Second Crusade, Duke Welf VI founded the Prémont monastery here in 1147, which remained in existence until 1803. The Roman-style façade of the minster represents the architectural style of the time when the Order was founded, and the priceless interior the various styles through the centuries through to the dissolution of the monastery.
In addition to the minster, which became the parish church of the little town, the only parts remaining of what was once an extensive complex of buildings are the west wing of the cloister (13th century, Gothic vaulted roof), the Brunnenkapelle (15th

century), and St John's chapel. This romantic circular chapei with its gothic vaulting reminds the visitor of the Chapel of the Holy Sepulchre in Jerusalem and has served since 1853 as the mausoleum of the Counts of Dürckheim-Montmartin. In the entrance hall (1491) to the minster are the remains of frescoes, dating from äbout 1600, when the church was painted. They show meinbers of the priricely family of Welf. Their burial-place inside the minster is marked by a metal plate in the middle aisle. Epitaphs are mounted on ihe pillars to the left-and the right for Welf VI (founder of the monastery, died in 1191) and his son Welf VII, who died young in 1167. They were produced by the Munich court sculptor Joharin Baptist Straub, and the excellent rococo work on the pulpit and the offertory (Anton Sturrn) date from about the same time, as do the pews and the confessional boxes and the ceiling paintings, which still impress the onlooker today with ihe freshness of the colours. Older items are the High Altar (1663), which in terms of style fits in between Renaissance and baroque, and the intricately carved choir stalls (1534). Other churches worth visiting are to be found in the outlying villages of Urspring (partly Roman-style), Kreuzberg, and 11gen (both 1564). The former plague chapel in Ilgen had to give way to a new building, built under the direction of Johann Schmuzer from Wessobrunn. A Picture of Grace stands on the High Altar showing the Mother of God and Her Child (about 1430).

On our way to the royal castles, we follow the B 17 along the edge of the Ammergebirge highlands, first arriving, after approx. 7 km, at the small holiday resort of Halblech, which consists of the villages of Trauchgau, Halblech and Buching.

Roman-style tower façade of the minster in Steingaden.

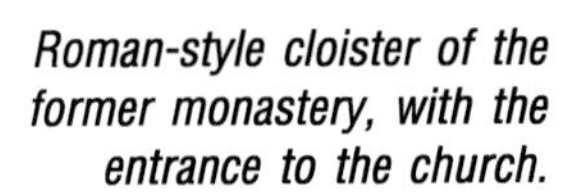

Roman-style cloister of the former monastery, with the entrance to the church.

Wieskirche: The entrancing volume of light flooding in through the broad window openings impressively brings out the overwhelming richness of form in the architecture, stucco work, paintings, and sculpture.

Tourist Information Buching:
Trauchgau, Bergstr. 2a, 87642 Halblech,
Tel. 08368/285, Fax 7221. internet: www.halblech-tourismus.de,
E-Mail: tourismus-Halblech@t-online.de

Halblech

The villages and their 3500 inhabitants are scattered across the naturally beautiful landscape between the Ammergebirge and the Lech River Valley with its numerous lakes. This makes for an extremely relaxed resort area in pastoral seclusion that still ensures convenient access to the main tourist attractions Steingaden/Wieskirche and Füssen/royal castles. Numerous recreational opportunities also make the place ideal for hikers and wildlife enthusiasts bound for the lakes (Bannwaldsee!) and the mountainous nature reserve in the Ammergebirge highlands, as well as for contemplative bon vivants. Even in winter, this resort offers an impressive array of sports such as skiing (cross-country and downhill), skating, sledding, curling, and snowshoe hiking.

We continue along the B 17 fort until we come to the turn-off "Königsschlösser" ("Royal Castles").

Schwangau
and the Royal Castles

Immediately after the turn-off, there stands the pretty pilgrimage church of St Coloman (1673) in the middle of a green meadow. Like its sister building, the Mariae Heimsuchung in Ilgen, the architect and stucco-master here was Johann Schmuzer. This church possesses notable late-Gothic carvings, and was named after an Irish pilgrim who rested here and is now honoured as the patron saint of farm animals; the Colomansritt takes place in Schwangau every year, and on 26th May, which is Wurmfeiertag or worms' holiday, there is a procession of petition to the church; the pious populace originally undertook to do this if the saint would relieve them of a plague of cock-chafers.

The pilgrimage church of St Coloman, with the first of the Alps and Castle Neuschwanstein in the background.

From here one can already see the brilliant white spectacle of Castle Neuschwanstein, one of the most fantastic and theatrical of all scenes. This is the intellectual creation of the mad King Ludwig II of Bavaria, known as the Märchenkönig or Fairy-Tale King, who came to the throne in 1864 at the age of 18. A good-looking but lonely monarch, he was enthralled by the world of German sagas and legends to which the musical dramas of Richard Wagner had introduced him. He withdrew ever further into his dream world, to which the castles also belonged which he built: Neuschwanstein, Lindenhof, and Herrenchiemsee: masterpieces of past history turned into stone. His tragic death in the Starnberger See, still to this day a mystery, put an abrupt end to his architectural efforts.

Tourist information: Schwangau Administration Office, *Münchener Str. 2, 87645 Schwangau, tel. 08362/8198-0, fax 8198-25,*
Internet: http://www.schwangau.de, e-mail: kurverwaltung@schwangau.de
Open from Mon. to Fri., 7.30 am to 12.30 pm and 1.30 to 5 pm; during the season on Sat. from 9 am to 12 noon and on Sun. and public holidays from 10 am to 12 noon.
Hohenschwangau information office: *open every day from Dec. to Oct. (closed in November).*
Schloss Neuschwanstein: *Open 1st April to 30th Sep. every day, 8.30 am to 5.30 pm; from 1st Oct. to 31st March every day from 10 am to 4 pm, closed on 1st Nov., 24th, 25th, and 31st Dec., 1st Jan., and „Fasching" Tuesday (Shrove Tuesday).*
Schloss Hohenschwangau: *open 15th March to 15th Oct. every day, 8.30 am to 5.30 pm; from 16th Oct. to 14th March every day from 9.30 am to 4.30 pm, closed on 24th December.*
St Coloman's church: *for exact opening hours and timing of conducted tours please phone 08362/8198-0.*

▲ The altar of the castle c

◀ Neuschwanstein with the Alpsee in the backgroun

Castle

◀ Living room

▼ Evening ligh

Throne room ▲

Neuschwanstein

Singers' room ▶

He ordered Neuschwanstein to be built from 1869 onwards, taking the Wartburg (in Saxony) as his prototype and setting it, a five-storied palace, on a wild, romantic cliff above the Alpsee and the Pöllatschlucht waterfall and decorating it richly with lofty rooms and slender towers. The magnificent residential and formal rooms are decorated almost exclusively with pictures and symbols from German pre-history, with the legendary figures of Siegfried and Lohengrin, Tannhäuser and Parzifal, and illustrations of the fabled singers' competition and the Meistersinger. The King exceeded himself in these extravagantly decorated rooms with the Sängersaal or Singers' Room, which takes up the entire length of the fourth floor and is a copy of Tannhäuser's legendary castle. From the western side the visitor can enjoy a magnificent view across the Upper Bavarian landscape of mountains and lakes.

From the car-park and bus-stop it is possible to reach Neuschwanstein on foot in about 30 minutes, or, for a small charge, to be transported up there by horse-drawn carriage. The sights worth seeing at the top include the iron Marienbrücke, which leads across the gorge at a height of 92 metres and provides a wonderful view of the 45-metre high waterfall.

The yellow buildings of Castle Hohenschwangau stand at a lower point on a wooded hill only a few minutes on foot from the car-park. This is where the Lords of Schwangau once had their family residence, built by Ludwig II's father,

Maximilian II, in the neo-Gothic Tudor style of an English castle. Here again, the Schwanenrittersaal (the „hall of the knights of the swan") is evocative of the Lohengrin legend, and this is where the young Ludwig II made his first acquaintance with the heritage of legends and sagas which were to become his world.

Castle Hohenschwangau: Rittersaal.

Winter romantic atmosphere on the edge of the Alps with Castle Hohenschwangau.

From the balcony of the Tasso room, Ludwig later stood with a telescope to keep watch on the progress of the building of Neuschwanstein.
In fine weather it is worth taking the cable car up the Tegelberg (1720 metres), an outstanding viewing-point from which one can see whole of the Alps and also an excellent start-point for walking tours through the Ammergebirge nature conservancy area. Otherwise, we can take the Schwangauer Strasse to the centre of the lively holiday resort of Schwangau (population: 3,600), which apart from the castles also offers the plain around the Forggensee, green hills, and rugged Alpine peaks, not forgetting the four lakes and an unspoilt, authentic town centre. Schwangau is the destination not only for hikers and cyclists, spa guests and kite-fliers, anglers and surfers, skiers and skaters, as it offers myriad possibilities and, in addition, Füssen is not far away (4 kilometres) - the last shining light along the Romantic Road.

Hiking by the Schwansee below Neuschwanstein.

Füssen

At the foot of the Allgäu Alps, the force of the Lech glacier in the last Ice Age created a charming landscape of moraine hills and numerous lakes. At about the time of Christ's birth, Romans conquered this area and opened it up with a military road, the via claudia (from Venice to Augsburg), securing the access to the pass with a castella (fort) on the hill now called the Schlossberg. In the 8th century, St Magnus worked as a missionary and teacher of the Faith in Füssen, where

Füssen, the centre of the eastern Allgäu, seen from the air. On the hill is the Hohes Schloss, and near the River Lech is the former Benedictine Abbey of St Mang.

Tourist information: Spa Administration Office, *Kaiser Maximilian Platz 1, 87629 Füssen, tel. 08362-93850, fax 08362-938520, Internet: http://www.fuessen.de, e-mail: kurverwaltung@fuessen.de*
Füssen Municipal Museum: *April to Oct., Tues. to Sun., 11 am to 4 pm, closed on Mond.; Nov. to March, Tues. to Sun., 2 to 4 pm, closed on Mon.*
State Gallery in the Hohes Schloss: *April to Oct., Tues. to Sun., 11 am to 4 pm, closed on Mon.; Nov. to March, Tues. to Sun., 2 to 4 pm, closed on Mon.*
St Mang's church, Spitalkirche, Franciscan monastery with St Stephen's church: *open every day.*

he died in 750. His monkish cell gradually developed over the centuries into the present-day St Mang's monastery with its church, in the crypt of which there is a fresco (about 980) representing St Magnus and St Gallus. In 1313, the town came under the sovereignty of the Prince-Bishops of Augsburg, and was then annexed to Bavaria in 1802. The former Roman military supply road had by the Middle Ages become an important trading route, and Füssen a transshipment point at which goods from Italy were loaded onto rafts. During the town's highest flowering, in the 15th century, the local craftsmen also profited from this trade, with the makers of lutes and later also of violins enjoying an international reputation. Füssen today, with its 16,400 inhabitants, is the shining star of the eastern Allgäu, and a central tourist location with a huge number of leisure activities at all times of the year. Just to take hiking and walking paths - they total 180 kilometres, and lead to all the beauty spots in the surrounding landscape and to chapels, churches, royal castles, lakes, and mountains.
The start-point for a circuit of the town is the Kaiser Maximilian Platz, where the Tourist Information Office is housed in the spa administration building. From here the Reichenstrasse leads through the middle of the old town centre, where the traders and craftsmen lived who gave the street its name: „Rich people's street". On the right, the façade of the Krippkirche fits into the row of houses which were built in 1717 - 18 to a plan by the great architect Johann Jakob Herkomer. This was also the time when the body of the missionary cross (Anton Sturm), the votive pictures, and the High Altar were produced, the latter probably by Dominikus Zimmermann, the creator of the Wieskirche. The name of Krippkirche, or Church of the Crib, relates to the picture over the High Altar. The

The Reichenstrasse with St Mang's church tower (left) and the clock tower

neighbouring building has a pleasing bas-relief showing a late-Gothic Madonna (about 1500).
The clock tower of the Hohes Schloss looks down across the façades of the Reichenstrasse. Built between 1291 and 1503, this castle served as the summer residence of the Prince-Bishops of Augsburg. The clock tower is graced by two oriole windows, one of which could be used for pouring unpleasant material onto the heads of anyone attacking the castle; the other, mounted across the corner, was a look-out point for the tower watchmen who had to sound a warning if fire broke out at night.
At the point where the Reichenstrasse widens out and looks like a market street there is an iron cannon ball in the wall of the former Zächerlhaus as a reminder of the day - it was 11th June 1800 - when Napoleon's troops bombarded the town. We now follow the slightly twisty street past the Rathaus to the castle entrance.

View across the River Lech to the monastery, with the Hohes Schloss above it.

Entrance to the castle, with tower of the monastery church.

After passing through the first gateway we reach the romantic „painters' corner" which has two particularly attractive sights: the sally port and a defensive tower with a pointed cupola. From here the long upward path inside the walls leads up to the first floor of the south wing. There is another fantastic view from the gate-tower room on the gable side of the north wing, which is adjoined by the Dreifaltigkeitsturm. Between the windows of the upper floor we can see the red-and-white coat-of-arms of Augsburg and of the builder of the castle (in about 1500), Friedrich von Zollern. The artistic Gothic cassetted ceiling in the Rittersaal dates from the same time; it can be seen as part of a tour through the Municipal Gallery and the Bavarian State Picture Collections.

St Anna's chapel: Jakob Hiebeler's „Dance of Death".

The remaining parts of the building, decorated with trompe-l'oiel paintings, now house the Local Court.

We can enjoy a fine view of the River Lech and the Alps from the Hohes Schloss. At our feet lie the buildings of the former Benedictine monastery of St Mang, the church (1701-17) of which was built under the direction of the local architect Herkomer.

As in the Hohes Schloss, the Roman-style church tower was decorated in about 1500 with trompe-l'oeil paintings. The appeal of the interior is the enchanting statue of angels (1719) by Anton Sturm and the gloomy crypt, a relic of the preceding Roman-style church. A fresco was discovered down here in 1950 that had been painted when the crypt was built some time before the Year 1000 and in some places is very well preserved. The extensive sequence of frescoes in the cloister is some 200 years younger; this part of the building is now mainly used as the town hall. The historically important rooms, however, now house the municipal museum of Füssen, and these include St Anna's chapel; here one can see the oldest representation of the Dance of Death anywhere in Bavaria, painted in 1602 by Jakob Hiebeler. The vistor reaches the courtyard of the town hall and thus the musem from the Lechhalde side, where the busts of the four great benefactors of the monastery decorate the narrow entrance: Charles the Strong, Pippin,

Füssen municipal museum: the monastery library.

Leopold of Austria, and Welf of Swabia. The showpiece of the present-day town hall is the magnificently painted and stuccoed Fürstensaal, in which concerts are held in the summer.
On the way back down to the River Lech we notice the fine Spitalkirche (1748-49) on the left, which possesses a rich baroque interior. This jewel of Swabian-Bavarian rococo was created by a local architect, Franz Karl Fischer. Opposite there is a plaque commemorating the former Lechtor, the gateway on the river side, and from where there is a fine view across the river and the roofs of the old town centre with the monastery and the castle in the background. From here the Tiroler Strasse leads to the suburb of Ziegelwies, on the Austrian border, and a good starting-point for walks to the royal castles (2.5 kilometres), to the legendary Schwansee, to the Alpsee which Ludwig II particularly loved, or to the Kalvarienberg with the neo-Gothic chapel to the Virgin Mary.
To the east of the old town centre there is a relic from the time when the town was enlarged, an attractive section of town wall with the Pulverturm or magazine, adjoined by the Alter Friedhof (since 1528) and the Sebastianskirche. Alongside the main entrance to this cemetery there is a grave commemorating the painter at the royal court, Domenico Quaglio, who died in 1837; his main work was the restoration of the old castle of Hohenschwangau. On the south side is the cemetery of the Franciscan monastery, built together with its church in the 18th century, and in the immediate vicinity is the Bleichertörle. This used to serve the housewives of the town as the exit to the Bleiche, the meadow where washing was spread out to bleach in the sun. The sandstone

Front façade of the Heilig-Geist-Spital church.

bas-relief with the double coat-of-arms bears the date of 1503.
Füssen is not only a historic old town; it lives from and with its magnificent landscape. The road westwards leads to the outlying villages of Bad Faulenbach, acknowledged as a curative spa with mineral and mud baths, and Weissensee, a picturesque resort on the banks of the eponymous lake. The other lake, the Hopfensee, is approximately the same size and boasts the spa resort of Hopfen am See, lying on a sunny slope above the water. Both lakes offer facilities for rowing, sailing, surfing, swimming, and fishing, as does the Forggensee, an artificial lake of 16 square kilometres created by damming the Lech. Together with the smaller lakes, Füssen alone has a total of ten lakes and is thus just as much an attraction in the summer for lovers of water sports as it is in the winter for those who love ice and snow. And in winter there are 50 kilometres of prepared hiking paths, there are ski-ing and tobogganing slopes on the Tegelberg (6 kilometres), cross-country skiing routes, the natural ice of the Weissensee and the Hopfensee, and - all year round - artificial ice in the skating stadium; in fact, all possible variations on the theme of winter sports.

Perhaps the most beautiful time of year in the mountains is the autumn, when the leaves change colour and the eye can see to the furthest mountain peaks, as here by the Weissensee near Füssen.

Neuschwanstein Musical Theater

The theater, which was built especially for the musical, is a perfect combination of classical harmony and modern design. Located near Füssen in a spacious park next to the Forggensee and below the royal castles, the highly elegant structure embodies a gallant promise of what awaits the guest behind the impressive portals.

With best view of the stage and optimal acoustics throughout the 1300-seat theater, crowned by a Royal Box with its own salon and food service – the theater and its numerous exhibits, light sculptures, and installations provides for a fascinating dialog between art and nature, fact and fiction.

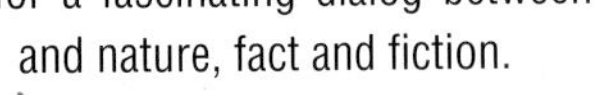